Working with Women's Groups for Problem Gambling

Why do so many women recovering from gambling addiction relapse?

Lifelong recovery requires much more than to just stop gambling. Women's groups provide long-term benefits and support and have proven to be highly successful in promoting recovery from gambling addiction. By following the story of a real women's group for problem gambling over the course of a year, Liz Karter explains how, for women, both the cause of and the cure for gambling addiction lies in relationship.

Karter shows clearly how learning to face and cope with real life situations and relationships is essential to maintain recovery. She shares the themes which run through each women's group, such as fear of trusting others, and the guilt, shame and risk associated with being truly seen and heard. *Working with Women's Groups for Problem Gambling* shows that with a combination of specialist intervention, women's group support, courage and compassion, women can learn to stop running from their addiction and instead find joy and support in building relationships and communities.

This highly accessible book provides a unique opportunity to gain a very personal insight into the group process, both for therapists and clinicians and for women wishing to better understand their addiction.

Liz Karter is a specialist in treating gambling addiction in women. She established and still facilitates the UK's first women's groups for problem gambling and is founder of the Level Ground addiction treatment practice. She is the author of one previous book, *Women and Problem Gambling* (Routledge, 2013).

Working with Women's Groups for Problem Gambling

Treating gambling addiction through relationship

Liz Karter

Routledge
Taylor & Francis Group
LONDON AND NEW YORK

First published 2015
by Routledge
27 Church Road, Hove, East Sussex, BN3 2FA

and by Routledge
711 Third Avenue, New York, NY 10017

Routledge is an imprint of the Taylor & Francis Group, an informa business

© 2015 Liz Karter

The right of Liz Karter to be identified as author of this work has been asserted by her in accordance with sections 77 and 78 of the Copyright, Designs and Patents Act 1988.

All rights reserved. No part of this book may be reprinted or reproduced or utilised in any form or by any electronic, mechanical, or other means, now known or hereafter invented, including photocopying and recording, or in any information storage or retrieval system, without permission in writing from the publishers.

Trademark notice: Product or corporate names may be trademarks or registered trademarks, and are used only for identification and explanation without intent to infringe.

British Library Cataloguing in Publication Data
A catalogue record for this book is available from the British Library

Library of Congress Cataloging-in-Publication Data
Karter, Elizabeth, 1966–
  Working with women's groups for problem gambling : treating gambling addiction through relationship / Liz Karter.
    1. Women gamblers. 2. Compulsive gambling. I. Title.
  HV6713.K37 2014
  616.85'84106—dc23
  2014007902

ISBN: 978-0-415-85961-5 (hbk)
ISBN: 978-0-415-85962-2 (pbk)
ISBN: 978-1-315-75829-9 (ebk)

Typeset in Times
by Apex CoVantage, LLC

To all my wonderful family and friends who are my supportive community, my group, who help make life more beautiful and at times when it is not are always there.

Contents

	Acknowledgements	ix
1	Why do we need Women's Groups for Problem Gambling?	1
2	Meetings in the first two months	21
3	Developing themes and relationship	41
4	Meeting halfway through the process	61
5	Working towards closure	79
6	Life after Women's Group	97
7	For the practitioner: starting Women's Group for Problem Gambling	115
8	For the practitioner: what makes a Women's Group therapist?	135
	References	151
	Index	153

Acknowledgements

My deepest thanks to the women of the Women's Group for Problem Gambling, London, who agreed to share their stories to make this book possible.

Thank you to all the women I have met with over the years that have contributed to my understanding of women and gambling addiction and been so endlessly supportive and encouraging of my growing the Women's Groups for Problem Gambling.

Chapter 1

Why do we need Women's Groups for Problem Gambling?

'It is all about relationship. We are all about relationship. Everything is about relationship. It is all about our relationship with others and our relationship with ourselves'. *That* is the answer I have finally formulated. Gambling addiction, for all its increased profile in the media, remains one of the least understood and one of the most misunderstood of all addictions. After more than 13 years of clinical practice in the area of problem gambling and specialising in women and gambling addiction and being asked, oh so frequently, 'So, what is it all about?', the answer I have just quoted is the answer that seems truly to capture the essence of what gambling addiction is all about at its core. Of course, you might be wondering if surely am I not over-simplifying things, and you would be right; and indeed there would be nothing else to write if gambling addiction in women could be summed up as neatly as that. And that is the thing; it *is* all about relationship but relationships are not neat and tidy. They are messy and complex and complicated and if we are engaging in them we are going to be feeling a whole lot. Sometimes we might feel joyful and exhilarating feelings and sometimes painful, anxiety provoking and depressing ones. As my first clinical supervisor once said to me, any close relationship is like a jam sandwich: it can be sweet, juicy and delicious, and equally messy and sticky and hard to clean up from; it can leave things stained and ruined.

The underlying motivation for gambling addiction, especially so in women, can always be found in relationship, whether it is in the 'too much' or in the 'not enough'. It is about having relationships that cause too much stress and pressure, are too demanding and leave a woman too exhausted to meet her own true needs, or relationships that have been damaging or, in the worst cases, abusive. Or it is about having not enough relationships, so that she is unsupported, lonely and isolated. Whichever it may be, the outcome is the same. When we scratch just below the surface of gambling addiction and the chaos of loss chasing and debt, the tangled web of lies that she has woven in an attempt to conceal her gambling and doing so also to protect herself from judgement and the shame that would come from having witnesses to the consequences, the woman with addiction to gambling is trying to cope with the negative impact of relationship. She finds that when she is gambling she is not thinking about anything else or anyone else. In that sense her gambling is self-soothing. A little win here and there might temporarily lift a low mood, but gambling *addiction* is not about winning money. It is about buying herself time out of her real-world experience, where the focus on the slot machine or the computer screen as she gambles online help her to feel in control, if just for that time, of her spiralling anxiety-driven merry-go-round of irrational thoughts and so too her stalking scare, her searing and relentless emotional pain, or darkly depressing feelings. These thoughts and feelings have been caused by her life situation, either in her current life, or by memories from earlier life experiences that are still troubling her, still influencing how she sees herself and affecting how she relates with herself and therefore with others. We find without exception that something about her relationships – past or present – has created a barrier to her healthy here and now relating, that she finds that she cannot ask for her needs and wants to be met, or set firm boundaries around herself, or is driven always to please others to the extent that she loses herself. Sadly, sometimes that loss of self has become almost complete to the extent that a mere spectre of a woman is all that is left in existence, with such a frail whisper of an inner voice as a guide for what is right for her that she can no longer hear it herself. All of these, and any of these, and a myriad of other fine details of the damage done by poor relating have left her mistrustful of being close, and so she is cut off from the many benefits of healthy relationship. Perhaps she has now forgotten what they were. Perhaps, sadly she has never experienced them. All she does know, although it may still be in felt sense rather than conscious awareness, is that gambling her troubling thoughts and feelings away feels like a safer option than the risk that experience has taught her is associated with being sufficiently intimate with another in order to express them. She is not gambling to take a risk, but to attempt to take emotional and psychological control.

The result predictably and paradoxically is not control but chaos. Unaffordable amounts of both time and money spent buying herself escape into the haze of gambling creates an additional set of problems. Her preoccupation with gambling means that focus on commitments such as work and any existing routine and okay relationships begins to fail. She grows increasingly secretive and withdrawn, constantly in conflict with rationally knowing that she has to stop gambling or the situation will worsen, and yet feeling that she cannot face life without it. All this creates additional anxiety, depression, isolation and loneliness. The only way to take control and to stop gambling is to stop running and to face her fears. These fears are of facing up to and managing the mess that gambling has now made; unmanageable debt, broken trust, painful truths yet to be fully disclosed to her, let alone to others. Underneath the layer of gambling are concealed the original fears that drove her running to isolate herself in the barren and limiting world of addiction. These fears are the hardest to stand and face because within them is where the pain and terror lies. Whatever lies there, she feared it so greatly that she chose instead to put herself continually through the miserable cycle of gambling addiction rather than to face these monsters.

The only way to take control is counter-intuitive; it is to stop running and to turn and face, and to confront, resolve and adjust. To do whatever it is that needs to be done. In order to do this she will need all the support and help she can get from good healthy relationship . . . and yet it is unhealthy relationship that triggered the use of gambling as a replacement for missing healthy relationships. Can we perhaps begin to see her dilemma? The antidote is made from what she feels has been her poison, and that is close relationship. That is why the findings of my clinical experience have been that encouraging women to engage in women's groups for problem gambling is difficult, but also why the women's groups I have facilitated consistently produce such satisfactory results for the women who do somehow, despite all their understandable fears based on their frame of reference for relationship, find the courage to attend. They are reversing the process. They are standing and facing their fears, learning what it is that needs to be different and how to make adjustments and to resolve; they are learning how to safely express rather than to suppress by gambling addiction. They begin to replace gambling addiction through the experience of the all-round benefits of belonging to a group, at first, and slowly, within the therapeutic group, but then expanding the learned skills to both give and receive the benefits in their world outside of the therapeutic space.

From the day we are born we belong to a group. The primary group of course is that of our family. Our family group is the root of all other group experiences. Being our very first group experience, and needing the care and protection of our family group in order to survive, we eagerly learn what we perceive to be our place in the pecking order, and observe the values and expected ways of relating within our family, which we use as material to write our own metaphorical 'Rule Book for Relating', which, although incredibly powerful, we may not even be consciously aware of, and so we may carry that book of rules, unedited, for a lifetime. The dynamics of the family relationships begin to write a script for the role that we feel we should play in order to be accepted in future group situations. Our family group not only hands us the set of rules for relationship and the script for the role that we are expected to play within group situations, but of course has a direct influence on many of the subsequent groups we may join. Our family signs us up for playschool and nursery, the schools we belong to, the clubs we attend in our recreational time. They perhaps sign us up for belonging to particular religious groups. More subtly, we are being enrolled into social/socioeconomic groups; we are being influenced early on by our particular culture, by those our families socialise with. We are none of us as a baby born with middle-class or working-class values; we learn these norms and values from what we see modelled to us by those around us. We take what we have learned as the group-appropriate morals, norms, values and aspirations and take them out into the world as our template for life. Often we then seek employment that reflects our learned group mentality. We leave home and create a home of our own, which makes a statement about the group we feel we belong to. Grayson Perry, in his recent television programme (Channel 4, 2012) exploring our predilections for particular interior design style, analysed the ultimate reason for our choice to be that of reflecting through our home environment a belonging to our chosen or aspired-to social group. So, be it a preference for bone china and Chesterfield or the latest minimalist style, we have still not moved far from the symbolism of the totem. We mark our territory, we make displays that symbolise the group we belong to, and by implication so too the groups we do *not* belong to. We are saying that we are the same as, or that we are different from.

We feel afraid of the difference. Difference brings with it something we do not understand and so brings uncertainty. Uncertainty is a condition that I have consistently witnessed throughout my practice as being amongst the hardest for any of us to tolerate, often triggering acute anxiety. If we are different we risk judgement from our chosen social group and deep within ourselves still fear the same things that we all have feared since the beginning of time: separation, rejection, abandonment and loss of the connections that help to form our identity but on a primal level help us to survive. Often both sexes are amused by the stereotypically feminine question that women might ask each other before a night out: 'What are you wearing?' If we examine that question in any depth however, we would usually find lying at the bottom the fear of being different from the others of our chosen social group. It is perhaps a question asked more by younger and/or less confident women who feel less able to stand alone, and asked less by more mature and/or more confident women who feel a strong enough sense of identity and have enough experience to know that standing out as being different does not have to risk annihilation by our group. We sense that alone we are vulnerable to attack, we have only our limited individual resources to depend on in lean times financially or emotionally. Alone we constantly run a higher risk of our destruction. If we think about it, even in our teens when we often so desperately desire to create our own identity as separate from our parents, we frequently just move on to join another group albeit of a different kind and display our separation from our family group, and our transferring membership to the group of our peers, marked through the fashion we follow, the car we drive, the music we listen to, the tattoos with which we mark our allegiance to a group or a set of beliefs. In the secular culture most of us now inhabit, our group identity is now more often reflected in the visible and the material. In the spiritual and religious world we have been gathering together for group comfort and security for thousands of years, taking comfort in having our existential beliefs and our fears witnessed and validated by others, being with others who are similar. If we belong to a religious group we are also handed a guide for life for times when our moral compass might steer us a little off course. We have a frame of reference and a framework for life, which is reassuring and frees us up from needing to make every decision autonomously and moment by moment as we can measure it up to the template given to us by our religion. Making independent decisions is a mixed blessing; it can feel wonderfully emancipating to be totally free to direct the course of our life, but with freedom also comes sometimes terrifying responsibility. For women, it is not so long ago that we were fighting for even the most basic freedoms, such as the right to vote. It can take very many generations to move into truly feeling a match for being responsible for huge life choices such as do we stay at home with children or have a high-flying career? Do we, as so many women have, try to have both? We find frequently that the latter choice often results in little time for supportive relationships, and to high levels of anxiety and depression. The Medical Research Council in Glasgow found that 38 per cent of middle class professional mothers with a degree reported high levels of stress, only slightly lower than those of women from more deprived backgrounds (*The Times*, 2013).

'Women are beginning to discover that nothing is more frightening than the escape into freedom' (Dowling, 1982). Within our group we feel we belong. We are the same as. If we are the same as, we are more likely to be accepted. If we are accepted by the group, we are more likely to be protected by it. Protection in modern western society is more likely to manifest itself in terms of approval and the maintenance of friendships and other desirable social relationships, but still through this sense of stability and security that it offers we feel stronger. Recently, we have marked the two-year anniversary of the London riots in 2011 when gangs of youths set fire to property and looted shops. The media pursued stories of those involved, revealing the backgrounds of some of the most serious offenders, and found consistently a lack of strong family group (Smith, 2011). Many involved were members of inner city gangs, where the skills of keeping good, healthy personal boundaries have never been taught by family groups and so are replaced by rigid physical boundaries marked by area and postcode and fiercely guarded. Where no strong sense of identity has been nurtured by family values and morals, any tiny graze to the self-esteem by another is experienced as a deep wound, resulting often in the wish to attack and destroy the other, the feared one who is different. However horrified we might have been with the actions of these gangs, does it not make sense that if, as we have discussed, one of our deepest fears is of not belonging to anything, such as a cohesive family group or a workplace relationship, that we choose to belong to *something*? It would naturally be easy at this point, with our tendency to wish to tidy things up and apportion blame, to aim that at the parents of the youth involved – the absent fathers, the irresponsible lone mothers. Yet the single mother at home is more than exclusively 'mother', she is a woman with needs for a support system herself if she is to do the best she can to raise her child.

> Just as children are absolutely dependent on their parents for sustenance, so in all but the most primitive of communities, are parents, especially their mothers, dependent on a greater society for economic provision. If a community values its children it must cherish their parents.
>
> (Bowlby, 1951)

Seventy-four per cent of women whom I have treated for gambling addiction over the last seven years have been single mothers. Often, they are found not only to be from a poor socioeconomic background but to have a very poor support network, and gambling to suppress their feelings has been a replacement for the avenue for expression that might be offered by the community John Bowlby describes above.

So when touching on the desire to belong to a group we are dealing with innate instinct. It is about survival and security and a defence against our existential fears of being ultimately individual and alone. We all know this to a degree, be it consciously or unconsciously, and it is reflected in so many aspects of our life from films about teenage cliques within high school and what happens if one is the overweight kid or the geek, through to Sartre's work *Being and Nothingness* (Sartre, 2000).

> Human beings seemed condemned to live in total isolation from one another, in the lonely grandeur of choosing for themselves. But in the critique it is specifically shown how human beings can by their own choice break down this isolation and form themselves into groups.
> (Warncock, 2000, p. xvi)

What, then, meets our instinctual needs in our ever increasingly frantic and secular world, where there is so little time for the coming together into group meetings of family and friends and religious gatherings, that might meet these instinctual needs? When the media fills us so full of fear regarding the threat to the safety of our children, should we allow them past the safety of the front door to go out to play and to learn about friendship and team work and community? We might answer that the coffee shop has become our gathering place. Certainly, it reflects more than a little of our instinctive tendency towards group mentality and our desire for routine and ritual that might go with our tribal instinct. We head for our preferred chain of coffee shop, often at the same time, the same day of each week; we seek out the familiar sign of our preferred shop if in a foreign town, seeking out the sense of identity, security and belonging that goes with group membership, not so much out of the need for caffeine (unless of course that has become a little addiction in itself!) but more out of the need to meet with others of our family and friendship group and to partake in the ritual it offers of slowing down, to sit with another, to listen and to be heard without the distractions of home or work life and technology. *Ideally* without the distraction of technology because we do not have to be at home or in the office to access the benefits and the pitfalls of a life lived online. To return to the question of how we meet our needs for group gathering in contemporary western culture, for the answer I would take the risk of saying that for everyone reading this book – and I include myself as the writer in this particular group – we need look no further than our pocket, bag or briefcase. The smart phone, the tablet, or the laptop contains instant access to our modern day social network. Our Facebook friends, the colleagues with whom we are LinkedIn, our Twitter feed, these become our social groups. How far does this *truly* feed us, however, and satisfy our natural longing to be a part of a group and a support network? Perhaps one way to answer this question lies in the recent reports of online bullying via social media. Within a two-week period we have news in the UK of women receiving threats of rape via Twitter and another teenage girl who committed suicide as the result of being bullied relentlessly by her peers online. Arguably, of course, this type of abuse has been committed by bullies and abusers since time began, but online perhaps it is easier to say what one would not say face to face *because* one cannot see the face of the victim? If we might include the reasons for the UK financial crisis and the role of the banker in this, it has been suggested that when trading became electronic, and therefore client contact limited, it became far easier to leap from necessary and appropriate risk taking to being reckless with other people's money and lives. It is far easier to bypass any empathy, to disconnect from feeling, if there is no physical evidence of the emotional pain and psychological distress. The effects of which have been proven to be no less than the physical act of violence or abuse that they may threaten, and in fact are the cause of the deepest wounds that never heal.

> Thus, although betrayal, powerlessness and stigmatization are integral to certain forms of sexual abuse, they are in fact psychological traumas arising from at least partially psychological events.
>
> (Briere, 1992, p. 24)

Counsellors and therapists who conduct online sessions frequently report that clients are quicker to a depth of emotional disclosure again because they do not have to sit physically with another who is witness to their pain and the shame that they might attach to it. This could be a great thing or this perhaps might be unhealthy avoidance of what ultimately is necessary if we are not to be eternally alone or to continually wear a mask that shows the fixed smile of 'I am okay' designed to keep enquiring others at a distance; that is, the sharing of our true self face to face and physically with another. As a client of mine stated when curious about online counselling, 'Oh dear, I don't think that would be very good at all. It would let me do what I like when I'm gambling – hiding. And that would not be good!' (Maddie, 48 years old).

If the contact offered by online social networking is of the friendly and social kind there are of course positives associated with this. It offers constant contact. It is consistent. The kind of friendships that are on offer are sometimes with those we never have actually met. We can invent and present a self we would like to be and hide what we consider to be our failings. We can communicate in shiny, humorous, superficial terms and so lower the risk of rejection that comes from deeper self-disclosure or more authentic ways of relating. We are able to connect with people internationally, crossing time zones, so when we wake alone in the night with a restless mind there is always another to feed us via Twitter with a word of wisdom or cheer. A life lived online can replace the need for the religious or the spiritual that is left by the trend towards secular society, with Google becoming our advisor; our guide to life available so easily at the click of a mouse and access to a search engine. And yet again I would ask, are we nourished by this sterile and dry diet of company?

> We can't say if constant use is good or bad. What is certain is that people need face to face contact. It releases bonding hormones that allow relationships to flower, and enables you to grow into a rounded being. If you live your life solely online, you are missing out on important chemical growth.
>
> (Felice, 2012)

As constant and consistent attachment to a relationship with others over the Internet may be, we are still, in fact, quite alone. The danger is that this diet of social networking can be just enough to take the edge off our hunger for belonging and for company. The quality of our social relationships in our 'real world' may suffer as a result of our preoccupation with virtual relationships and so, feeling increasingly isolated and alone, we turn more and more to cyberspace to meet our instinctual and oh so earthly needs. A few months ago whilst in a coffee shop I saw a scene that one might see anywhere on any day. Two women were sitting opposite each other, saying nothing. One woman silently wept whilst the other held her hand and handed her a tissue. No words needed to be exchanged at that time. So much more was being said through the language of the body and the expression in the eyes of each woman. Yes, we might replicate this with a video camera online, or with the 'sad face' emoticon, but what about the physical reassuring, soothing warmth of another's hand? What about the other to pass us the tissue, which silently says 'I witness your pain'? Have these things of the physical world become superfluous? Are they no longer a part of our instinctive needs? Or perhaps dangerously, we are just becoming less conscious of our natural need for such contact. With fewer opportunities to practise real relationship, we are becoming ever less able to manage the degree of emotional intensity that accompanies it. Among other problems, we are in danger of addiction if we are to lose our social skills such as managing to deal with difference and so conflict resolution, and then so too our ability to risk being in close relationship. In his book *The Blind Giant* (Hardaway, 2012), Nick Hardaway speaks of how online relationship enables us to associate only with those who agree with us.

A report commissioned by the government's Chief Scientific Adviser, Professor Sir John Beddington (BBC Online, 2013), states that we will be spending an increasing amount of our lives online, causing a blurring of the boundaries between our virtual and real-world identity. Working so closely and extensively with addiction I fear for the possible outcome of this. What I have learned, as I stated at the start of this chapter, is that life in essence is all about relationship. Our lives are about our relationship with ourselves and others. If our relationships are to be increasingly conducted online, we are in danger of losing the ability to relate with ourselves, if our focus is always on what to post, how to promote ourselves or on digesting the steady flow of information that is drip fed to us via the Internet 24/7. There is little time and space to listen to our own thoughts and to tune in to our own feelings, both of which are equally 24/7 sources of information about how our life is going at that time and what we might need to adjust.

> With excessive use we start to define ourselves by our external output, rather than from within ourselves, our own robust identities. You have a very shaky sense of self if it constantly needs external feedback. And, if you're constantly outputting data, when do you have time to think or reflect?
>
> (Newman, 2012)

It is interesting to note that the limited time to think and reflect is one of the very things that appeals to the woman who gambles excessively on slot machines or online.

The findings of Dr Ethan Kross, psychologist at the University of Michigan, are that Facebook actually undermines wellbeing. There was a correlation between the more time users spent on Facebook and a worsening of how they felt (Kross et al., 2013). Research from the University of Chester, in which participants kept a 14-day contact diary with six communication modes, found that people were happier and laughed 50 per cent more with face-to-face or Skype contact than when using non-face-to-face methods such as social networking sites, instant messaging, phone or text (Vlahovic, Roberts, & Dunbar, 2013).

Our interpersonal real-world relationships and situations will suffer, as potentially we lose the ability to sense what is being said in nonverbal communication such as body language and eye contact. We are in danger of losing confidence in presenting to the world anything other than our 'I'm okay', 'smiley face' self. In doing so, ultimately the danger is losing essential life skills such as the ability to deal healthily with confrontation, conflict resolution, to be able to feel empathy, to experience the courage to have our voice truly heard and to risk witnessing the expression of sadness, disappointment and/or anger that it might evoke in the other. We lose the opportunity to experience the learning that, no matter how acute the pain of separation and loss in real-life relationships may be, we need not be destroyed by it. These things might be possible to practise to an extent online, but the key is in the witnessing. To witness the *full* experience of another and to have our experience witnessed in return. To take the risk of sharing the same physical space with another and to risk their judgement of us, to risk the pain and anxiety of separation and loss that are the flipside of the golden coin of the attachment that we all so deeply desire to earn, even if owning it might also be our greatest fear. I fear that less engagement in real-world relationships will result in the tarnishing or virtual loss of these vital skills. I fear that if this is indeed the result of increasingly life being lived out on the online world, and of our belonging to social groups where we might have hundreds of 'friends' but not one person amongst them with whom we would trust with our truly authentic thoughts and feelings, that we will become more vulnerable to addiction. I have seen each day since 2001 the result in the treatment room of withdrawal from real life and relationships. Our natural and instinctive need to connect with some*one* is replaced with absolute connection with and absorption in some*thing*.

Research found that four out of five students suffered mental and physical distress including feelings of panic, distress, confusion and extreme isolation when forced to be without technology for one day (ICMPA, 2010). Almost 1,000 university students interviewed at twelve campuses in ten countries including Britain, America and China reported cravings, anxiety and depression and they felt they would not voluntarily be able to give up their technology.

Constant access to those we feel attached to online denies us the valuable opportunity to learn to cope with being separated and so heightens our anxieties at times when we are forced to be so. If we remove the essential ingredient for gambling addiction – that of course being money – the description of the students would be that of the experience of the woman addicted to online gambling or slot machines going through the excruciating early phases of withdrawal. It is a painful separation from that with which she has been inseparable. A symbiotic relationship is created with gambling behaviour, that sense of no boundary between where the self begins and ends and the other starts and finishes. Total preoccupation, a build up of unmanageable debt, and worsening relationships all combine to cause depression and anxiety, which may have been initially eased by gambling, to escalate. She feels less able than ever to cope with her more intense thoughts and feelings and therefore less able to manage the necessary practicalities of day-to-day life. She withdraws further from any healthy relationships she may have for fear of having her gambling discovered and so having to give it up. As much as she detests her dependency on it she fears losing the escape route it offers. Her shame and guilt leave her fearing being cast out from her family and social group and so she hides by exiling herself. The outside world, which was initially for her a hostile environment, feels now even more threatening.

And so our need for attachment is always present and we will meet those needs in the best way we can. Ideally, we meet those needs through healthy groups of family and friends or, if they are missing in our lives or if we are too busy to make time to gather together for support or if we are fearful of being so close, we are perhaps drawn to social groups online, or by attachment to the activity of gambling. I have often found that for women whom I meet with addiction to online bingo, that initially one of the most attractive aspects of the online gambling site was that it offered membership to a group of friends. The advent of social gaming and games played on social networks such as 'The Simms Social', provides a significant link between social networking sites and gambling or gaming. These social games might be free to play, with charges only for premium content, but I have known women cross addict to these games whilst going through recovery, and there may be no money to lose, but what about the cost in preoccupation, lost time and focus on real-world relationships?

> **'I realise now I was playing the Simms six hours a day, because I was so lonely and it was like a family' (Rhianne, 46 years old)**
>
> A survey by the UK Gambling Commission revealed that 55 per cent of women questioned had gambled in the last month. Twelve per cent had gambled online (Gambling Commission, 2013). GamCare released statistics to show that, in 2012, 35 per cent of calls to their national helpline were from women. Fifty per cent of those women had a problem with online gambling (GamCare, 2013).

For the woman who is isolated and lonely because of her mental health problems, such as depression and anxiety, or for the woman who fears the consequences of meeting physically with others, here offered within her own home is the opportunity to ease her loneliness without ever having to take the risk of truly being seen and heard. Or for the woman who is too exhausted after her working day to spend time with family and friends, or has neglected these due to her career and so equally outside of the workplace is isolated and lonely, her social life comes to her through the computer screen. This could indeed now be any woman, from any walk of life. Online gambling has nimbly leaped the social divide. The Adult Gaming Centre (AGC) arcade or bingo hall ten years ago might have been frequented by predominantly working-class women; online bingo is just as likely to be favoured by the middle-class professional, on her Smartphone, on her tablet, on the commuter train home. She, like all other women, is screened for that time, from all the natural stresses and anxieties that come with life; balancing her finances, deadlines, her children's play dates, but sadly too she is shielded from all of the many all round health benefits that come with physical meeting for fun and support.

Here, in this chapter, I am aware that we are focusing heavily on the woman who gambles online, as we explore the damaging effects of fragmented social groups in the physical world and the poor replacement we are offered via the Internet. For the many women who historically have been, and indeed the very many who still remain traditional slot machine players in the AGC, arcades and in bingo halls, they frequently describe their social needs being met in a similar way. They might be in an arcade surrounded by others, but the focus on the machine leaves them feeling at the same time very much separate and protects against unwanted engagement with others. In the arcade they are able to feel a sense of group belonging, a shared purpose and identity, their need to be in the physical presence of others being to an extent met, but with no true meeting of minds or authentic selves to be risked. The arcade staff, if they are welcoming to them as regular customers, offer a sense of friendship or even that of a substitute family, but again without the risk of crossing too many personal boundaries. It is easier to remain in control of which aspects of oneself are revealed and to feel in control of these more superficial relationships, which can be left in the arcade when they return home: to limit who enters their 'real world' and so who sees their 'real self', in just the same way as the women who gamble online can shut out their world of online friends when they press 'shut down' on their computer.

Perhaps in addition to the virtual world, we also have the added difficulty now with the general western world view of the desirability of independence. Women are told about the empowerment they will experience if they no longer need a mate, and earn their own independent income. Even certain schools of therapy can convey the message that to be dependent is a negative; it is a mark of failure, with associations to being unattractively weak and needy. Whatever we do, do not 'need' another or others, we are told. It is a backward slide to the hearth side! Again, if we may look at the work of John Bowlby, some of which was drawn from his many years of experience as a weekly facilitator of a London support group for young mothers, he was keen to be clear that attachment does not indicate a regression but performs a natural, healthy function in adult life as well as childhood (Bowlby, 1951). In contemporary times, magazines and newspapers are strewn with studies indicating that women are not as happy as we were told we might be or indeed *should* be with our new-found independence and empowerment. Perhaps having been given so many messages that we should be thrilled with being able to 'have it all', we feel less empowered with the right to say 'Actually, being able to have it all does not mean I want it all, because I still have to do it all and it leaves me exhausted!' How dare we be so ungrateful?

> The problem is that they have sprung out into the world, but they have not really left the house.
>
> (Dowling, 1982)

Pull between desire for independence and stability is normal. In this book we shall see as the chapters unfold that this ambivalence, this swing between the polarised, but each equally magnetic position of dependence and independence, manifests itself in Women's Group meetings from the point of very first contact, to early attendance at meetings and arising again and again throughout the process. Being in close relationship with others raises these issues for all of us to one extent or another and even more so if life experience has shown us that we cannot depend on another to take care of us and our more fragile feelings. To aspire to be entirely independent, or completely dependent, or indeed to attempt the delicate balancing act of resting somewhere in the middle, is a decision we may not consciously be aware of making. Our choice may depend on life circumstances, our desire for any of these positions may alter as our life circumstances change, as our life experience such as marriage, children, divorce, bereavement, and the aging process brings us changing evidence of the benefits of being in either position. None of the life positions from dependence to independence are necessarily unhealthy places to be. What is healthy is that we feel we are making our choices to arrive at any of our chosen destinations as conscious and considered decisions. And, that we are making our choice freely and not out of fear. For the majority of women who are members of Women's Group they have made their choice out of fear. Fear of being dependent on another because they have experienced the sickening feeling that accompanies betrayal by someone close whom they should have been able to trust. Some women fear the risk of independence, believing that they will not survive the world without another to make decisions for them, to be their voice; they have no belief in an even faint sense of their power as adult women, and relate to others and the world from a childlike position of deference and passivity. The consequences for women who have chosen either way of being, based on fear, have been the same. That they have each suppressed the voice inside, which quietly pleads for either company and support, or a means of true self expression and room to grow, and have done so by gambling themselves into a place where the view of their inner and outer world is so hazy that they can no longer see what it is that they are missing or would truly choose for themselves if they were not paralysed by fear. The close relationships that are grown within Group, the witnessing of others who have made similar fear-based choices and are seeking the freedom that is desired and feared in equal measures, will allow the silenced inner voice to begin to be heard. If they can allow themselves first to face the fear of being close and belonging and yet still maintain their individual and autonomous self they stand a chance of beginning to make a free choice regarding where they truly wish to stand in the eternal balancing act between independence and dependence.

Women's Groups for Problem Gambling, the first of which I established in 2006, grew organically out of the need which became apparent as I listened to the women I met with in treatment for gambling addiction. They would report feeling disappointed with their uncomfortable experiences attending the predominantly male support groups that were on offer. Gamblers Anonymous do hugely valuable and very admirable work, but women consistently would speak of it being an almost exclusively male group. Their discomfort at this was primarily for three reasons. The first reason being that when it came to the practicalities of the chosen mode of gambling – at that time, the majority of women with gambling addiction were traditional slot machine players – or the sought after experience, such as escapism through absorption and preoccupation causing a numbing of thoughts and feelings, they did not feel understood by the male members of the group. More than one or two of the women would speak even of being mocked by male problem gamblers, who accused them of not being 'proper gamblers' because they did not place bets, or seek a buzz from their gambling. This may, if taken on surface level, seem like an 'excuse' and 'avoidance' of seeking help and support, but if we bear in mind that 84 per cent of women who have attended women's groups I have facilitated have a history of child abuse or have experienced domestic violence, perhaps it will then give us a little empathy with how difficult it might be to have – what they rightly or wrongly perceive as – experiences of men abusing their power or position. As one woman, with a history of being abused by an uncle as a teenager and as an adult desperately in debt due to gambling, manipulated into sex for money by a male family friend, described her experience: 'I felt bullied by this one man, so I didn't say anything else in that meeting. I don't want to go back' (Clare, a slot machine player for 15 years, 49 years old). Women who have survived such experiences frequently live by the rules of 'Please others', 'Be good', 'Don't tell', amongst others, which they have found equally help them not to rock the boat because they have a much better chance of surviving life if they are compliant and pleasant. They are unlikely therefore to feel able to verbally defend themselves, or to be emotionally robust enough to withstand such challenges.

The potential problem with peer support groups where there is no group therapist is also that there is nobody there to challenge the validity of a woman's perceptions. It might be quite true that she is being mocked, bullied and silenced by a man in the group. It may be equally true that because it is her experience that men have treated her so, that she has become hyper-vigilant to these experiences recurring and so is quick and sensitive to interpret maybe even more innocent interactions as threatening. As much of this will be out of her awareness, as it has become so automatic and essential to her living safely, it is beneficial to have a group facilitator to help her to shed light on what is truly going on; both in her inner dialogue and that which she is having with the other group member. This is another piece of the puzzle that I was fitting together, which would eventually begin to look like an effective women's group for problem gambling.

The third reason, which is by no means the least important by virtue of it being mentioned last, is that as I was learning through extensive experience, and by listening to the often painful and shocking stories that women were sharing with me, it was essential to offer a form of treatment to address the underlying motivation for gambling addiction. I was treating many women with histories of cross addiction, who had been jumping from one stepping stone to another in the form of drugs, alcohol and then gambling, all in an attempt to cross the raging torrent of the river that had become their life. Many women too were presenting with co-morbidity such as self-harming behaviour, for example cutting and burning, or eating disorders including both anorexia and bulimia. The term 'self-harm' I found to be misleading as, again, like the gambling addiction, these other behaviours, as ultimately harming to the physical self as they might be, were in fact distractions from the emotional pain and psychological distress that sufferers found to be the most insufferable. The self-harm was in fact an attempt at survival when the self just could not take any more. The reason for this pattern of cross addiction and co-morbidity, being more often than not the root cause of these issues, was almost always one and the same for all of their coping mechanisms, had never been identified and addressed. Frequently, the root cause would be buried in deep, dark areas of life experience such as abuse of a sexual nature or domestic violence, meaning that there would be very sensitive and intimate issues to gently uncover and explore, and many women felt that this was not something that they would wish to do, or would feel was appropriate to do, in a mixed-gender group. Even without these sensitive issues to take into consideration, men and women generally have very different experiences of upbringing, socialisation, and therefore being, in relation to the world. When such a damaging consequence of gambling addiction is the destruction of the ability to engage and relate with others, to provide a space where it is as relatively easy as possible to begin to do so, because a woman feels as safe as possible and that she might be understood by others of her gender seemed to make absolute sense.

If I may take us back to the start of this chapter, at the risk of repeating myself, I believe it is a risk worth taking to say again that gambling addiction always makes sense on some level. No woman is gambling addictively because she truly believes that she will have a life-changing win, or because she is greedy, or irresponsible, or does not realise that the odds are against her, that she will not emerge a winner, but will ultimately destroy her emotional, psychological and physical health. She is gambling at all costs because the world outside feels intolerable to her. She is gambling because her inner world of thoughts and feelings is out of control, wildly unpredictable and acutely painful. She is gambling to attempt to feel calm and in control. One of the things of which we are least in control is the behaviour of another. I began to see this pattern of fear at this realisation spreading through all of my work with gambling addiction and women. Themes were developing as women spoke of their fears of relating intimately: the fear of the monsters that their minds created as they imagined the horrors that would accompany becoming close; being out of control emotionally and the fear that close relationship with others potentially was the hair trigger to fire off what they found to be deeply distressing feelings, such as those of uncertainty, separation, loss or fear of betrayal of trust. Working with the underlying issues for gambling addiction was already an established part of my practice at that time and I worked with a strong relational focus to the therapeutic relationship, finding that providing the women I met with, with a sense of my being more of a real person rather than a more traditional blank screen created trust in the therapeutic relationship and provided a means of practising how to relate with others in the world outside. Key life skills that are needed to live a healthy life, but are lost under gambling addiction and the more years that a woman has been gambling, the harder they are to find. Often I found that I was in a re-parenting role as the original family had failed to impart healthy relational skills. The result was so often that as we peeled back the layers of, first, the smothering layer of debt and chaos, then the gambling behaviour and the underlying motivation for it – damaging relationship experiences – we would find a frightened, lonely, childlike self of a woman, keeping herself physically isolated, or with a myriad of ways to avoid true intimacy with those she was in proximity with. She did not trust others and did not trust herself to be able to maintain healthy, flexible boundaries, to be able to discern who to allow in close or who to keep right out. She may have learned to trust in me as her therapist, but what about out there in the wider world? Encountering people whom she could not be assured would withhold judgements and behave appropriately, because it was their professional and ethical duty? What if others were to hear her darkest secrets, the things that still filled her with guilt and shame that were the consequences of her desperation to gamble? This is where the double bind would tie her up to a place where she could not move forward in recovery beyond using sheer will power not to gamble. Isolated and lonely, she was left still depressed and anxious; still was vulnerable to gambling to escape from the trap of loneliness or her troubling thoughts and feelings because there was no support for them.

Often, where we are so afraid to try something that we are frozen to the spot, once we have identified what that fear is and why it is there, the only way to make a change in our 'stuckness' is to take the risk of having a go at doing the very thing we are afraid of doing and, hopefully, this time having a positive experience. We experience that the bad thing that we thought might happen, or has happened in the past, does not have to happen again. Or, that if it does that we are different now, we are perhaps stronger, more resilient, better able to deal with it from the position of our adult self. The women I was working with needed to take that risk of relating and beginning to experience that there are in fact some people who could be trusted and, vitally, that they could trust themselves to take care of themselves in close relationship and not allow themselves to slip back into old patterns of becoming lost underneath the needs of the other. There was a need to have a safe space to practise developing the skills of being involved in what they most wanted and needed, but what they most feared: close, supportive relationships. The very first Women's Group for Problem Gambling was born, replicating a family, friends, school, college, the workplace. Any group situation that the woman might have encountered would be remembered, either consciously or unconsciously, with expectations of receiving the same experience, the same treatment, thinking, feeling and reacting in the same way. This was a chance to do something different, to challenge through here and now, experience expectations of what it means to be in truly intimate relationship. As we shall see as we now move on to follow the story of one group over one year, from beginning to end, it is indeed a challenge, but one that is hugely rewarding if she can find courage within herself to take what is to her the biggest risk of all, that of being fully within relationship.

Chapter 2

Meetings in the first two months

Women's Group for Problem Gambling, which we will be following, started in October 2012 and met weekly for one and a half hours on the same day, at the same time and at the same London venue each week. The group consisted of six group members with me as Group therapist. The maximum number of members in each Women's Group never exceeds seven women. I have found that this number is enough to create a varied group dynamic and for it not to feel too intimidating as a smaller group might where the attention is necessarily more focused on the individual. In a group of seven it is possible to get one's voice heard and be a presence in the group but equally it is possible if one so chooses to remain, if not entirely invisible, out of the spotlight and in softer focus. Remembering that most women who come to Women's Group do so after long-term gambling addiction, and that the consequences of this include severely damaged relational skills, means that it takes time to build trust in the group process, in the Group therapist and especially in the other Group members. I have found that if a woman is allowed to move forward naturally into finding her voice in Group at her own pace it is much more productive than if she feels overly challenged. If she feels intimidated or is challenged too soon, it not only risks her shutting down, as this has been her familiar response to challenge, but risks losing her entirely from Group. The group process can anyway be very challenging in terms of the content of material and the intense emotional processing that is entered into once trust has built and a cohesive group has grown; because of this I prefer to invite into Group only women who have experience of either previous group therapy or one-to-one therapy or counselling. This issue will be explored in more detail when we go on to look at the suggested assessment process in later chapters, but for now it is important only to note that my experience has been that on any occasion when I have invited into Women's Group a woman who has not experienced counselling or therapy, no matter how carefully I have attempted to explain what the process of Women's Group might be like, she has invariably been taken by surprise by the stories that she hears told and by the intensity of emotional expression that she might witness being attached to the stories. Again, having suppressed feeling with gambling for perhaps many years, she may intellectually understand that in Women's Group she will do so much more than talk about gambling behaviour; that the agenda is not only to explore what it is that motivates the behaviour, which is usually distressing thoughts and feelings about disturbing life and relationship experiences, but to begin to understand how she might *feel* about doing so when she has not felt anything of any significance for so long is a huge leap. My experience has been that women who come to Group unprepared to think psychologically and to express emotionally do not stay in Women's Group and my concern would be that they might be discouraged by what they perceive as a negative experience of therapy from seeking therapeutic help in the future.

Women who become Group members make a commitment to weekly attendance, with the exception of illness or planned holidays. The weekly commitment is to allow each woman to get the maximum benefit from the process. Because of the relational focus of the group the maximum benefit will only be gained if relationships are developed, and for this to happen there needs to be regular contact. If the group begins and is not already at maximum membership, or if a group member leaves before the end of the life of Group at one year, then a new member may join at any point until there are five months left for Group to run. If there is less than five months left, it is not long enough either for group dynamics to adjust to the new member or for the new member to benefit from the group process. Potentially, it might be damaging as she may uncover issues that she then has no time to process within Group before closure.

Following careful consideration and through experience I chose to allow new members to join throughout the life of Group. This is because, as we discussed at length in Chapter 1, gambling addiction is about difficulties in managing life and relationship. In order to reverse the process of withdrawing from both, Women's Group is a safe space in which to practise developing healthy relational skills. To be in healthy relationship with others, or to even allow ourselves to begin to take that risk, we need to be able to manage our feelings that are evoked around issues of attachment, separation and loss (Bowlby, 1986). In essence, Women's Group should replicate as closely as possible: the issues we deal with in relationship in the world outside; how we feel when we begin to get close to and attach ourselves to another; how we feel when we are separated from another;

how we feel at the loss of the relationship we took the risk of allowing ourselves to build. If within Women's Group there are experiences of these life issues, for example as sometimes the loss of an established member means the need to begin to trust and attach to somebody new, we are replicating as closely as possible life in the world outside of Group, where if we are to truly live a rich and varied life we need to be able to manage our feelings around meeting new people and saying goodbye to those who have become familiar and of whom we are fond. These thoughts and feelings evoked in Group can be identified and the anxieties around them made conscious as fear and so each woman has a chance to explore her individual response to fear: is it fight, flight or freeze (Bradford Cannon, 1871–1945)? Women's Group, if it is working well and healthily, should become a microcosm of life and relationships outside, with all the fears, hopes, fantasies, support, companionship and sadness – and yes, I have seen tears of laughter too – that we will encounter. These are the ever present thoughts and feelings that we essentially need to be able to encounter and to ride and survive if we are not to remain isolated for fear that what we think or how we feel in close relationship will destroy us, and through our self-imposed imprisonment remain, lonely, anxious and depressed and so ever vulnerable to addiction.

Let us now meet the women who together formed the Women's Group for problem gambling that we are to follow. I wish to emphasise at this point that the names of the women have been changed to protect their identity, and although all events that are described to have taken place within Group are true, any identifying facts of life and key people in the women's lives outside of Group have been altered where necessary, again to protect the identity of the women we are about to meet who so kindly gave their consent to have their stories told for the purpose of this book.

Paula

Paula is 49 years old, lives alone and has been unemployed for 15 years since suffering a breakdown. She has never been married but has had a few long-term relationships with men, the most significant of which sadly ended in the death of her partner through heart disease and, afterwards, Paula miscarried their child in early pregnancy. Paula has support from mental health services, with access to a care coordinator and has in the past been hospitalised with both voluntary and involuntary detentions. Paula has a seven-year history of gambling online and before that of severe self-harming behaviour, including cutting and burning herself on a cooker or with an iron. In her early years, Paula grew up within a large family with both mother and father and was one of four sisters and one brother. From the age of seven years, Paula was sexually abused by her cousin. At the time of arriving in Group, Paula had already been in one-to-one therapy with me for 18 months and, while having significantly reduced her gambling, found that she was still vulnerable to relapse, with psychological and emotional triggers that we had identified, but that she was actively working on being able to defuse with distraction techniques and by making adjustments to her day-to-day life to make it more rewarding and satisfying to her.

Helen

Helen is 46 years old and lives with her same-sex partner of seven years. Helen has been within the mental health system with periodic times of needing to access increased support for diagnosed Post Traumatic Stress Disorder since being raped by a man ten years ago and has been unemployed since that time. In her early years, Helen had experienced a great deal of disruption and little stability, with several house moves and her father regularly moving out of and then back into the family home. She has one older brother with whom she now has little contact. With an addiction to slot machines, which began after the rape, Helen at the time of beginning Group was struggling to maintain any consistent gambling-free time and had began to gamble online at home, which had caused an escalation both in her gambling and in her debt. Helen had received one-to-one therapeutic support within two other agencies, but was disheartened with what she felt to be either a focus exclusively on the gambling behaviour, or scared by what she perceived as too intense or too quick an exploration of the rape she had experienced.

Terri

Terri is 42 and is married with two grown up daughters in their late teens. She has a diagnosis of borderline personality disorder but, despite the difficulties this presents her with, she is able to work and enjoys her job within an office environment. During her early years Terri grew up with both parents and one younger sister. Terri was regularly psychologically, emotionally and physically abused by her mother, which, she believes, was with the knowledge of her father, who did not intervene. Terri had spent two years in therapy with a male therapist to address issues related to the abuse. Six years later, on entering one-to-one treatment with me she had a five-year gambling addiction to slot machines, which she is now largely in control of with very occasional relapses.

Janet

Janet is 38, a single parent of five children and is unemployed, having never worked. The children have two different fathers, but neither she nor her children have contact with either father. Originally from Trinidad, Janet experienced much disruption and separation with her mother leaving her to be brought up by her grandparents from the age of five years old and never having known the identity of her father. Janet has a history of cross addiction from alcohol to crack cocaine and when she approached me for treatment for gambling addiction had a six-year slot machine problem. On entering Group, having completed one year of one-to-one therapy with me, Janet is established in recovery from problem gambling and is regularly in attendance at Narcotics Anonymous and Alcoholics Anonymous meetings. Janet has no contact with any family members and her only social life is through her active involvement in her local church. She is currently involved in a court case to regain custody of her two youngest children who are in foster care following accusations of neglect whilst she was still gambling.

Sarah

Sarah is 44, married for 25 years and has two sons in their early twenties who still live at home. Sarah has been unemployed for two years since suffering a breakdown and before that time held a responsible, professional position within a large company. In her early years, Sarah was unhappy at home due to her overly strict parents and so left home at 15 years of age, found work and was self-supporting until her marriage at 19 years of age. She has contact with her sister and shares care with her of her elderly mother; her father died several years ago. On entering Group Sarah had minimal experiences of one-to-one therapy, having attended 'Relate' for two sessions with concerns about her marriage. Sarah has an addiction to online gambling, which began when she had to give up work owing to her poor mental health. When first entering Women's Group her gambling was still out of control and she reports that if she has available funds she is actively gambling on a daily basis.

On the morning of the first group meeting I arrived as I would normally 45 minutes before the start of the Group meeting in order to prepare the group room. This was a light and airy room with plenty of space potentially for the seven chairs that might be needed for the Group members plus of course one for me. The chairs were placed in a circle with enough space between each to ensure that personal space was honoured and that accidental physical contact was limited, whilst equally not so much space that it was not possible to make physical contact with another if both parties so wished. In the centre of the circle was a circular coffee table on top of which was a box of tissues, a jug of water, plastic cups and a plate with two types of biscuit. The room itself was decorated in light colours with abstract paintings on the wall. There was no window and air conditioning provided temperature control.

> *Twenty-five minutes before the start of Group at 11 o'clock my mobile telephone rang, and when I answered I heard Paula's voice in unusually panicked tones explaining that she had followed the map she had downloaded from the Internet three days ago and yet, despite this careful planning, had taken the wrong exit at the train station and was now still some distance away and fearing she might be late. I reassured her of the directions and that it was okay if she arrived a little late, that the important thing was to arrive safely.*

Paula's anxiety around being late was in stark contrast with her usually organised and in control self that she presented to the world. I was mindful of the fact that this journey was taking her not only out of her comfort zone physically, as she tended to keep to a rigid routine and familiar environment, but that the result was her feeling out of her comfort zone psychologically and emotionally. This was something that I anticipated would be the experience of all of the women who were journeying in for their first Group meeting. Let us remember that gambling addiction, far from being about risk and recklessness, is an attempt to take control of overwhelming thoughts and feelings and offers a sense of the predictable in terms of the repetitive behaviour and predictable, if painful, feelings that are the consequence of it. Those thoughts and feelings may be painful in the extreme, but at least they are familiar. What is unfamiliar, uncertain and therefore scary is life outside of that comfort zone of addiction. The journey that she takes on that first day of Group is a courageous one as she travels to meet the unknown, new people, a situation where she will feel she has little control.

> *At just before 11 o'clock I went to the reception area to meet the Group members, as we had agreed. Terri, Janet and Sarah were all seated in the waiting area. As I greeted them and they got up to follow me through to the group room, Paula hurriedly came through the front door, obviously flustered and highly anxious, keen to let everyone know that she had downloaded a map days ago but that it had wrongly directed her. Despite there being no sign or word from Helen, we walked through to the group room and chose seats.*

Noticing where each woman chooses to sits is of value, especially if noted in relation to the location of the door. Some women choose to sit near to the door, preferring to feel safe in the knowledge that they can exit easily if they choose to. Women who are the survivors of abuse or domestic violence frequently prefer to sit facing the door and may be disturbed if seating arrangements require their back being to the door. Life experience has shown them it is wise to be vigilant to who may be entering their space. It is equally worth noting details such as does she choose to remove her coat or keep it on? If she removes it, does she put it out of her way, or does she sit clutching it to her, or folded on her lap? Both of these can indicate that she is feeling anxious and is either ready to leave if she gets scared or is using the coat as a physical shield against anticipated emotional and psychological discomfort.

I noticed that none of the women present chose to sit with their backs to the door and all took their seats with a little talk about the difficult journey that Paula had experienced. As everyone took their seats there was a firm knock at the door and Helen entered the room, apologising loudly and profusely for being late; she too had downloaded a map that had given her the wrong information. She explained her difficult journey with much humour, which the group were quick to respond to, as it was in all likelihood a way of relieving some of the stress and anxiety that they felt at being in the meeting. We shall see as we move on that humour was a way that Helen would tend to dilute the intensity of certain situations within the group process. It seemed that all Group members were keen to join in the discussion of the problematic journeys and described in detail each route they had taken. This might either be seen as avoidance of getting started with the therapeutic process, or equally as a welcome opportunity to seize an early opportunity to be the 'same as', an early bonding opportunity and so a chance to be accepted as someone whose journey also was difficult. Metaphorically of course this was a rich symbol for exactly the life journey each woman had been on, which had led her to be in that room on that day. Life itself had thus far proved a very difficult, and in many cases perilous, journey.

Before any new Women's Group can start it is essential to discuss the group contract. This will be outlined in more detail in Chapter 7, for clinicians, later in this book, but for now it is important to know that the contract is an informal agreement between therapist and Group members and comprises common sense and issues that clinical experience has taught me most frequently arise during the life of Group. The issue with which most women are primarily concerned is that of confidentiality. The woman who is taking the courageous step of becoming a member of Women's Group is ultimately going to be revealing aspects of herself that have remained hidden from others for some years. The identity of problem gambler is a label that covers the true identity of the woman whose life has been affected by her addiction. It can be a label that feels shameful to wear, but at the same time safe by comparison. It effectively conceals all that she feels ashamed of underneath; the effects of her gambling addiction on others and on herself and the stories that tell of what triggered her gambling. When she has gone to such lengths to keep all of this hidden, it is going to take courage to begin to peel off the label and to begin to tell the stories that have been hidden for so long. In order to make a start, she is going to need reassurance that her story will be heard and held in confidence by myself and other Group members and not told in the world outside. Because the nature of my work means that I might write and speak about my practice I am always careful to state that I do not tell any woman's story without her express permission. We need to remember at all time that in order to reverse the isolating process of addiction that is withdrawal from relationship, healthy therapeutic relationships need to be established, and in order for this to happen, just as with any relationship, the cornerstone is trust.

In this first meeting of this new group as ever the only group 'rule' that I asked everyone to stick to very closely was this:

> *With the exception of physical illness, however you are feeling, come to Women's Group.*

This is simple, but I have found it carries so much meaning and importance and I have found has gone as far as to save a group member who is wavering in her courage from gradually missing a meeting here and there, to missing two in a row, to gradually letting go of her at first tenuous attachment and drifting out of what is often in the early stages a so very fragile process. The subtext of this simply worded rule is, if I may quote the title of the popular self-help book: *Feel the Fear and Do it Anyway* (Jeffers, 1997). Gambling addiction, indeed any addiction, blocks out our ability to feel; that is the intention, either consciously or unconsciously, we wish to avoid feeling our inner pain. When a woman begins to become free of gambling, she frees herself up to feel again. This can be wonderful as she feels all the joys and pleasure of life that have also been numbed, but also terrifying as she begins to feel all that she was running to addiction to avoid. It is at these times that she may in the early stages of Group wish to avoid attending Group meetings, as in doing so she hopes to avoid confronting her unsettling reality and feelings about it. There is so much to be gained from those times when she comes to Group, despite her fears. As we shall see in this book, it is a richly rewarding opportunity to identify just what it is that her gambling has been helping her to run from. Running from Group, running into gambling, are one and the same thing: a fear of feeling, be it anger, sadness, shame or guilt. If she can get herself to Group and begin to stand and face it, she begins to break the cycle of taking flight triggered by fear. As I add to 'the rule', even if she comes and does not wish to say anything other than 'Liz, I really don't want to be here today' (and yes, that really does happen), it is at least a step in the right direction of acknowledging the existence of the feared feelings and beginning to share them honestly and openly with herself, even if she is not yet ready to share them with Group. To be able to sit with and to tolerate our pain is an essential life skill if we are not to spend a lifetime taking flight and avoiding our inner world, and our inner world responses are triggered by outer world situations and vice versa. One of the purposes of Women's Group work is to learn these essential life skills and to broaden abilities to go out and be adventurous explorers of both our inner and outer worlds. So, therefore, yes, a small and simple Group Rule, but with potentially universal significance and importance.

Checking in

Checking in is something that each woman is invited to do at the start of each Group meeting, and at the end of each meeting she will be invited to check out. Checking out is a summary of her thoughts and feelings about the group experience that day, a chance to consolidate, debrief and feel to grounded before going out into the world. Both checking in and checking out also provide a kind of self-assessment, which can be encouraging and give her faith in herself and the process to reflect on positive steps forward that she has taken. Essentially, checking in offers her a few minutes to focus on herself, to summarise how her week has been, to tell of any significant events, any thoughts and feelings that have troubled her, or have been pleasurable. All of these may help to identify triggers to gambling. If she begins to pick up patterns such as an argument left her feeling angry but feeling unsafe to express her anger, she suppressed it with gambling. Or feeling upset left her feeling tearful, but crying scares her because she feels vulnerable and so she gambled to build a dam to stop the flow of her tears. Most often I find that the early stage group check in is predictably made from safe topics, such as reported gambling behaviour or facts about living and work situations, with the perceived risk of any more intimate thoughts and feelings carefully avoided. It consists much more of a description of what she does, and much less of who she truly is. After all, in the early groups, she is likely to have verbally made a commitment to the group process but, in terms of how she feels about it, maintains an understandable ambivalence. If she is not too sure if she will return next week, let alone whether the other members she is just meeting will, why would she share intimately when she needs to prove that her stories will not be carried off and scattered carelessly outside? When, despite the contract to listen and treat each other with respect, she is not sure she will not be judged and attacked for what she shares? After all, the likelihood is that if she has tried to talk about her gambling in life outside of Group, she will have received harsh criticism from those who do not understand gambling addiction who have told her in no uncertain terms that she should just stop, that she is never going to win. She may be in a group of women with a gambling problem, but what if nobody else has as severe a problem as she does? Or what if they have worse problems and think she is making a fuss over nothing? And perhaps, worst of all, can anyone else possibly ever have behaved in the way that she feels is so shameful in their desperation to gamble . . . ? Let us hear how the first check in was managed by the Women's Group we are now following.

> *I explained the process and purpose of checking in and that as this was our first meeting it would be good if each woman would say as much or as little as she felt comfortable with at that stage about her life outside of gambling and what it was that she would like to get from the Group meetings, other than stopping her addiction to gambling.*

Setting what we might call a personal agenda has the benefit from the outset of encouraging each woman to begin to think about herself as an individual who might be the same as others in the group in many ways, including of course in that she has a gambling addiction, but might too be different in terms of wants and needs. For the woman who finds it difficult to get her voice heard, her agenda might be to practise speaking out in Group. For the woman who always uses humour to dilute the intensity of a situation, her personal agenda might be to allow herself and others to sit with a depth of feeling. Almost all women I have met come to Women's Group having lived life by the rule of 'Please others'. Often high on the personal agenda for these women is to practise the art of now and then putting themselves first, by taking the time they need to talk in Group, not being distracted from their own issues by picking up those of another group member. The personal agenda also encourages from the very outset thinking about what it is that is difficult about relating in life outside of Women's Group. It both instils and reinforces the idea that Women's Group is a space in which to practise life and relational skills to take into the world outside of Group. Even from the start of Group the focus is on expansion following the suffocating constrictions of gambling addiction.

> *I encouraged that, whilst anyone was speaking, other members listened without interruption. As in each meeting I left it to Group to decide who should begin the checking in process, rather than proceeding one by one around the circle.*

When a high proportion of the women who attended Group have experienced abuse by those with power over them it is important to create from the outset the sense that they are empowered to make their own choices within Group. For the Group therapist, this also allows an opportunity to learn about how much space each woman feels she is entitled to, how comfortable she is with being given permission and with giving herself permission to have her voice heard.

> *Helen took up the invitation to check in first. She appeared agitated and nervous, but spoke for around five minutes, giving her first name and talking about her gambling addiction and how she felt that at present it was beyond her control. She shared that she had been taking out credit cards and using them to gamble online and that her partner was aware of this and it had damaged their relationship. I noted that Helen seemed careful not to say anything that might reveal that she had a female partner, perhaps wary of how this might be received by Group. I noticed that she would quickly glance at me when she referred to her partner, perhaps keen to check that I would not give away what she wanted to keep secret at this stage. Bearing in mind that Helen had had limited contact with me beyond brief telephone calls to arrange appointments and an initial assessment for Group membership, in that sense she had no reason to trust me, anymore than she had reason to trust any other of the group members and in some ways perhaps even less reason. At least with the other Group members they had their common identity of gambler to create the reassuring 'same as' connection. Helen spoke of how*

gambling had stripped her life bare of the creativity that used to enrich it. She used to love to paint and to play the guitar, but she had had no creative urge since the all consuming urge to gamble desensitised her desire to experience anything else. Helen mentioned her involvement with mental health services, again diluting the intensity that she imagined this disclosure might have created by saying, 'But don't worry, I'm not mad, well not too bad really!' The other Group members seemed relieved to be rescued by her humorous ending to introducing herself and responded by reflecting with laughter. I asked Helen was there anything that she wanted to get from Group other than to learn how to stop gambling? She replied that she wanted to know why she gambled, that she had not learned from behavioural therapy what the triggers were for gambling and that she just felt deep within herself that she needed to understand what triggered it in order stop gambling in the long term.

None of the other Group members offered any other reflection on Helen's check in. Janet then began to speak.

Janet's position as an experienced group member was evident as she spoke with more confidence in her voice and with more openness about her background of cross addiction, her regular attendance of anonymous meetings and the fact that two of her children were in care and that she was involved in a court case to regain custody. She closed her eyes as she asked God to forgive her for neglecting her children and to show mercy and see that she was doing all that she could – with his strength – to remain free of addiction and to make positive changes in her life. I wondered what other Group members might think of Janet's being so strong in her religious faith and of her tendency to speak openly and directly to God. I had experienced this in our one-to-one work and it no longer surprised me, but I was aware of feeling surprised by it at first. I noticed Terri watching her closely. With her negative experience of being abused by her own mother, it would be unsurprising if she was watchful for any signs indicating that she might need to be on her guard. Perceived difference often creates a sense of fear in any of us. Janet then spoke of her concern for being for the first time in Women's Group rather than a mixed gender group. 'I don't like women, I don't trust women. When I first met Liz, I told her I didn't think I would stay with her, but she was alright', she said looking at me with a knowing smile and moving her foot closer to me (we were sitting side by side). I remembered well Janet's initial reluctance for us to work together and was touched by her both speaking and demonstrating warmth *towards me now, but also wondered how that might be perceived by other Group members.*

Having previously or currently worked with some women who attend Group and not with others can raise issues of insecurity and jealousy among Group members. Women who are not in one-to-one treatment with me may envy what they imagine as a special closeness that I share with a member I currently see or have seen for one-to-one therapy. They might fear what is being discussed in one-to-one therapy: is the group member speaking negatively about them to me, or am I as the therapist sharing information that I am privileged to know about one group member with another? These can be viewed as problems and potential barriers to effective work being done, or as the potential for each woman to learn more about herself and how she is in relationships where care and attention must be shared. It is an opportunity to actually overcome potential barriers to close relating, such as fear of feeling the mind-twisting, knife-sharp pain of jealousy, fear of the sickening feeling of betrayal. I have therefore learned again through extensive clinical experience that there are enormous benefits to having worked with, or still to be working with, in one-to-one therapy a woman who is also in a group that I am facilitating. One of these benefits is that I am of course aware through our one-to-one therapy what her particular issues in relationship are. Being in Group together, where she is in relationship with others, means that I will see these issues in action, I will be aware more quickly than I might be if we worked together only in Group of what might be being played out between her and another group member. Although it would be inappropriate for me to raise in Group anything that she may have disclosed in our one-to-one sessions, or indeed to discuss another group member's issues in her one-to-one therapy, if she raises issues she has with another group member or with the group process in general, what I *can* do is help her to understand the meaning of what is going on for her on more than a surface level, and encourage and support her in addressing the issue in Group, in her relationship with the relevant group member. If she can begin to do this within the safety of Group it is a step towards doing similar in relationships outside of Group. I can help her to understand the basics of what is known in therapeutic language as 'transference'. This means that whoever we are, no matter how good or bad our life experiences and experiences of others, we all carry certain expectations based on how we have been treated by others in the past into our here and now relationships. So, if we use Janet and Terri as examples, both women had experiences of their trust being betrayed by their mothers. Therefore, any women they might get close to in life – regardless of age and ethnic background – might in some ways, and not even conscious ways, represent their mother. They therefore would be likely to *transfer* all of their past experiences of mothers into their relationship with any other women and respond to them accordingly. If viewed from that perspective, does it not make complete sense that Janet might not trust women? If she could not trust her own mother to keep the promise she made her to come back to get her from her grandparents, how might she trust any other woman? And yet, slowly but surely, she had learned to trust me. Being in Group was a huge step forward to facing her fears of being in relationship with women and so potentially opening up her world to all of the comfort, support and company that might be available to her if she could begin to allow herself to take her place in the wider world of adult women: 'for centuries, women have formed passionate, close friendships, as women's private letters and diaries attest. These relationships have emphasized self-disclosure, emotional closeness and empathy, and have often been a core part of women's emotional lives' (Lips, 2006).

> *Terri was next to check in. She began addressing Janet directly, saying that she could relate to her views on women, that she also found it hard to trust her own gender. She said too that she could not imagine what it must be like for Janet to have two children taken away from her, because she herself 'lived for her two daughters' and had been very careful to protect them from the kind of experiences she had lived through as a child. I was aware of the dynamic that could be in action, that perhaps, to Terri, Janet was representing her own abusive mother. I wondered how it might feel for Janet to hear her comments, might she feel judged? Terri then went on to describe her own situation in more practical detail, the details of her gambling behaviour, the debt, the problems it was causing her marriage. She then suggested that Paula take over.*
>
> *Paula appeared surprised by Terri addressing her directly. I was aware from our one-to-one work that Paula tended to live by the 'Please others' rule and, although she was working hard at effecting change regarding this in her day-to-day life, I was aware that in the early stages of Group, when under pressure and in new relationships within which trust was yet to be established, it was natural for most women to regress to old ways of behaving to ensure they were okay. For most women I work with, their Rule Book for surviving life would read in bold type 'Rule Number One: Please others'.*

> Paula did just so and although I could see she was not yet prepared to check in, she began to talk about her gambling behaviour in detail. As had everyone else, she was hiding behind the tough shield fabricated by gambling talk. I noticed too that Paula was using a clipped, professional, emotionless tone, which we had identified in one-to-one helped her cope emotionally in stressful situations outside of Group. Being in her 'professional self' helped her to feel capable and to remain rational and so could be a helpful coping strategy, but of course to relate in any depth in Group she would need in time to put down this coping mechanism and to allow herself to connect both intellectually and emotionally with others. Given the challenging circumstance, her challenging journey and life journey, I am sure we might all see how it might be natural that Paula might want to draw on her professional self to shield her more vulnerable feeling self on that day. Paula also spoke openly and in detail about her involvement with mental health services.

Open talk about experiences with mental health services I have noticed is not at all unusual amongst Group members. In just the same way that the label 'gambler' can create a reassuring badge of shared identity to gain acceptance into a group of 'gamblers', so too can wearing the badge of 'mental health service user'. Being a mental health service user might create an automatic bond with other mental health service users in Women's Group, and in most groups there are frequently women who have support from mental health services and are on regular prescribed medication. The badge of mental health service user, just like that of problem gambler, also helps her to hide her true self and delay revealing to herself and to others the identity of the woman who truly lies underneath. Women who have had experience of mental health service groups or in one-to-one support may need extra encouragement to disclose things such as an increase in anxiety or a depressive mood because they may have expectations that this could result in reports to their mental health team, which might result in a hospitalisation.

> Sarah was the last to check in. She began to share her current situation, telling us that her day was dominated by her gambling, when she was not gambling she was preoccupied with gambling. She told us that she was miserable and that her husband who was very ill with arthritis was supportive in terms of being keen to help her manage her money and to take over the family finances so that she did not get into additional debt, but that all of that only made her feel worse.

> *She felt like a helpless child. She felt so stupid, having been someone who had been a high flying professional in the world of business who could not now be trusted even to buy groceries. Sarah began to weep and to apologise for that, because she 'did not do crying' but there was something about hearing everyone else's stories that made her own experience feel all the more real.*

Many women find that in the early stages of group therapy they are unable to experience in any depth their own feelings about their situation, either past or present. Gambling has been effective in achieving exactly what they wanted it to achieve and that is to numb and suppress any uncomfortable feelings, and the subsequent devastation it has caused also has been distraction. Guilt too often provides a firm stopper in the bottle neck of suppressed feelings. Frequently, when they first come to Group women feel that they are undeserving of any empathy for themselves, especially so if they have not had one-to-one treatment, which is aimed at identifying the reasons *why* they gamble addictively. Behavioural focused therapy or no therapy at all means that they come along to Women's Group feeling that they are stupid, selfish or are hopeless cases of addictive personality. They believe that the consequences of their gambling behaviour on others deserve punishment. They will not have 'excuses' made for their behaviour, behaviour that makes no sense to them themselves, so why on earth, they imagine, should it make sense to others? What I have often seen is that those very same women are moved to tears when they hear the tragic stories of other women, they are able even in the early stages of group work to pick up the threads of understanding for and therefore compassion for other women in their group way before they are able to follow those threads back and weave them together into the beginnings of understanding, compassion and so towards forgiveness for themselves.

> *Sarah spoke of how she had stopped speaking to her husband about her feelings because he did not understand when she spoke about having strong cravings to gamble. She said that one thing which she was aware of was that everyone else had had one-to-one counselling or therapy, whereas she had not. This concerned her because she wondered if group work would be enough for her, but she wanted to try, to see if she could get by with group work alone, because she felt in one-to-one the focus just on herself might be too much.*

We will see as we follow the process that for Sarah independence is particularly important. She had already of course described a life where she was used to being in control; she had been an authority figure at work and at home the financial provider and the carer for her two sons and her husband. It must feel uncomfortable for her to now be in the position of the power balance shifting at home. She had implied that she felt her husband was taking advantage of having power and influence over her; this, combined with her childhood experience of controlling parents, would make it understandable if she might then expect the same from others and no less from me or another therapist. Why would she then wish at this early stage to take the risk of being in a more intimate one-to-one relationship with a therapist, who usually is perceived by any client as an authority figure?

> *As Sarah finished checking in to the warm acceptance of her tears by the other women, who encouraged her not to apologise, that they understood just how hard it felt to begin to face the mess that gambling has made of life, Helen appeared agitated. She spoke across the other women, saying 'I am worried now, I think I've said too much, you see'. I asked her what it was that she felt had been too much. She replied that she did not know. It just felt like she had said too much. 'I'm not used to talking about it, you see'. I asked how she was feeling, right at that moment, having shared more than she was comfortable with, and she described feeling anxious. I shared with Helen and with Group in general that this was a natural response; that gambling is all about keeping everything inside and cutting off, becoming isolated, and then it can feel uncomfortable to begin to do the opposite at first.*

The Transactional Analysis (TA) Injunctions (Berne, 2010) describe well the 'Rules' for life that women who gamble addictively have been living by. Frequently from childhood, and sometimes in later life, they have found through experience and observation that behaving in certain ways around others guarantees them the best chance of avoiding disapproval and punishment, and ultimately ensures the best odds of surviving life.

TA identifies the following injunctions:

- Don't be.
- Don't be who you are.
- Don't be a child.
- Don't grow up.
- Don't succeed.
- Don't do anything.
- Don't be important.

- Don't belong.
- Don't be close.
- Don't be well (don't be sane).
- Don't think.
- Don't feel.

Along with these injunctions or Rules, TA identifies six 'Drivers', which influence our thoughts, feelings and, essentially, drive our behaviour.

1 Please others.
2 Be perfect.
3 Be strong.
4 Work hard.
5 Hurry up.
6 Be careful.

We, all of us, have recorded inside of us some of these rules. We started making inner tapes of all the messages we have been given by our parents, teachers, religious groups, peer groups and wider society from the moment we were able to observe which behaviours gained us the approval of others; it was a way of our survival. As with most issues of thoughts, feelings and behaviour, and of mental health, we are all of us somewhere on the spectrum. To have a volume control that we can choose to adjust on the Drivers can be good and healthy. For many women who attend Women's Group, however, the volume is deafeningly loud; they do not feel they can choose to turn down the volume, fearing that something bad will happen if they do – or if they break one of the Injunctions – one of the strict, suffocating and life-reducing rules that they have been taught to live by. This often has created a life so restricting and miserable that one of the functions of gambling to distraction has been to drown out the more authentic voice deep within when it begins to scream to be rescued from the trap of a life the woman has found herself in. With Helen, we see an example of this. She came, as do so very many women, living life by an additional and strict 'Don't tell' rule for life. Her authentic voice began to come through when she perceived herself to be in a safe space in Women's Group, but having broken the rule by beginning to 'tell' she quickly felt anxious about that. Bad things happen when we break rules, we learn early on as children. A battle women face early on in group work is a battle within them; to take the risk of becoming their authentic Adult selves and expressing themselves through their own true thoughts, feelings and behaviour whilst battling with the little girl within them that fears the consequences of breaking the rules they have lived by. All too often they have had good reason to feel such fear. A woman's Adult self might rationally know that she is in a safe environment, but unconsciously, she will transfer her childhood feelings and experiences onto all others in Group and automatically respond as she did to survive as a fearful child.

The first Women's Group meeting, of 48 meetings in total, sets very much the pattern for the process of meetings for the first six to eight weeks. As we can see, the women who were in the process of becoming new members of Group cautiously tested out relating as yet on a superficial level with an emphasis on talk of gambling behaviour and its impact. All had experienced damaged trust in relationship throughout their lives and we see them relating very much from safely behind the mask of 'problem gambler'. This mirrors their lives outside of Group, where gambling addiction has helped them to hide from what they feel is the *real* risk: that of intimate relationship. The therapist's role at this sensitive time of building a cohesive group is primarily to do no harm, to remember that in their hands they hold the fragile, fledgling trust of each group member, that just as each group member fears being exposed and seen and judged, each member is closely watching not only every other member in Group, but also the therapist for any signs that she may betray their trust as others have before. It is vital at this early stage for the therapist to warmly witness and to work out what it is that each woman is hiding from behind her mask of problem gambler, but without tearing off her mask and exposing her true self before she is ready to risk being more truly seen.

Chapter 3

Developing themes and relationship

We ended Chapter 2 at the beginning of the process of building relationships within Group. During that first meeting we saw how much of the self-disclosure related to what each woman had been 'doing' rather than what it felt like 'being' her and discussed how there is good reason for wearing a mask of problem gambler whilst trust is being built in the group process. Just as she has been hiding from the reality of a life inside the haze of gambling, she hides behind the mask of problem gambler to hide her real self. Wearing that mask also has the added benefit of rendering her the same as the other members in the group. Being the same as, we are less likely to provoke judgement or attack, and so this increases the likelihood of forming attachments to others in Women's Group but still in a remote way; this too for the woman who has been gambling in the AGC or arcade and enjoyed the sense of being physically around others but not connected on any psychological or emotional level of intimacy. For the woman who has been enjoying playing online gambling games in which she plays with or meets with a community online, repeating that illusory sense of being close, but remaining remote. Just enough human contact to take the edge off a raging hunger for human company and to prevent her from taking the risk of going out into the world and finding true friendship.

I have learned to be careful to ensure that Women's Group does not become a substitute for this particular element of gambling addiction, mentioned above. The first meeting, which we read about in Chapter 2, described the pattern for relating for certainly the first six to eight weeks. If Group is working as it should, however, trust in the process and in each group member, and indeed in me as Group therapist, begins to grow. This nurturing and gradual growing of trust is an absolutely essential part of the process if a woman is to begin to take off her mask. A little like the allegorical children's story of the sun and the north wind placing bets on who could persuade a man to remove his coat, ultimately it was not the harshness and full force of the north wind, but the gentleness and warmth of the sun that did so. As this trust builds, and a closeness begins to develop between Group members within the group environment, it is natural that the warm and friendly feelings that are created are like rain to the desert of loneliness and isolation that is both her inner and outer world. It is natural too that she should want to bottle these precious drops and take them with her into life outside of Group, and hurrah because that is exactly what an enormous part of the aim of Women's Group is. The art is to take the skills that are learned in Group for how to be open, to have flexible personal boundaries; how to make friends in the world outside of Group. The difficulty is that feeling hard because in the world outside again it is about uncertainty and risk. It can feel hard and harsh to discourage intimate friendships to develop inside Group and to be pursued outside of Group, but clinical experience has shown me many potential dangers inherent in this for the group process as a whole, as well as for the individual women who do so, as we shall explore in this chapter. One of the very few Women's Group 'rules' that I am always keen to emphasise is: *Women's Group is a safe space to learn HOW to make friends, not to FIND friends for life outside.*

So, how is it possible that the women we left in Chapter 2, fearful of being in the same room with another, can have been on a journey within eight weeks – and let us remember that that is in total a mere 12 hours – together that has led them to a point of feeling trust enough to feel genuine attachments begin to develop along with a genuine desire for friendship?

I believe that working with the core conditions of Carl Rogers' Person-Centred Model (Rogers, 1951) of Congruence, Empathy and Unconditional Positive Regard are invaluable as the bedrock for Women's Group therapy.

- *Congruence (genuineness)*. I have found that to be a real, live person capable of thoughts and feelings about what is happening in relation to others in Women's Group in that moment encourages others to begin to be open with their own immediate experiences. If we bear in mind that many of the women who attend Group have good reason not to trust in relationship and have frequently been betrayed, we can understand how they might have negative associations with secrecy. I have found that one disclosure often is returned with another, so if I am seen as someone who can tolerate, for example, feeling sad at hearing the painful story told in Group, then that often encourages a woman to attempt to sit with her own sadness, rather than suppressing it, as she has done with gambling. If I am asked a question about how I feel in that moment in Group I will answer congruently. I begin then to be seen as someone who is to be trusted. So too this applies to each and every member in Group. The more transparent each member is, the more this encourages the trust of each member in her, and trust in themselves to take the risk of being open with their true thoughts and feelings and not receive the judgement or punishment that she might have been taught to expect, if what she has said does not 'Please others', for example, or does not obey the 'Don't tell' rule.

- *Empathy.* The ability to empathise with another is something that I have never yet had to demonstrate to any woman in Women's Group. In fact, far from what is often perceived as typical character traits of the woman who gambles in shocking media headlines – selfishness and greed – are in my experience the polar opposite. As we touched on in the previous chapter, women who gamble addictively are usually doing so to hide from the misery and pain caused by living an inauthentic life of 'Please others', 'Work hard' and suppressing their true wants and needs. Their ability to empathise with the situation, and indeed with the motivation of others to gamble. is apparent very often from the first check in at the very first group. This experiencing of being heard and understood in depth, rather than judged at surface level again facilitates trust in becoming increasingly open. My role as Group therapist is to demonstrate empathy and to help a woman have self-empathy; to enable her first to give herself permission to go beyond the block of guilt at her gambling behaviour, so that she might better understand herself. If she can begin to understand *why* she gambled in the way that she did, she can begin to forgive herself, which is essential to the process of recovery, when guilt, regret and self-recrimination can all be strong psychological and emotional triggers for relapse.
- *Unconditional Positive Regard (UPR).* As with congruence and empathy, UPR is self-perpetuating. What an enormous amount of courage it takes each woman to tell her story in Women's Group beyond the surface level of gambling behaviour! The consequences of gambling behaviour can be shocking and it is not at all unusual for stories to be told of theft and prostitution to fund gambling; to hear of child neglect, as we have already the beginnings of, in the telling of Janet's story in Chapter 4. We shall hear more of how the stories of how gambling began can contain even darker themes of

experiences that the vulnerable inner Child of each woman has survived, or how her love and trust as a woman has been betrayed and attacked and abused on all possible levels. To reach this deeper stage of self-disclosure is essential if she is to fully make sense of why she so eagerly put herself into the cruel grip of gambling addiction and so understand better what her situational, psychological and emotional triggers for gambling are. This path will feel a less threatening route to negotiate if she has already experienced that respect for her is not conditional on her behaviour. That attempts will be made to understand why she did what she did, even if the behaviour cannot be condoned by a particular group member, this will build trust. In fact, on occasion, the negative response to a particular disclosure from group member A by group member B actually can plant a seed of trust in group member A. She might feel that she can trust enough in group member B to tell her the truth as she sees it, even if it does not please her to hear it.

The Person-Centred core conditions that I have here outlined are a constant in my practice as Women's Group therapist and I have found them to be consistently rewarding in building trust. A paradox is that, initially, many women do *not* trust in this approach. It is important that we remember that although gambling socially and for fun has associations with risk, gambling *addiction* in women is an attempt to take control by escaping from an environment that is perceived as threatening through the absorption of gambling and to take control of thoughts and feelings that are tortuous to endure. The woman affected by gambling addiction has therefore lost trust in herself and her ability to make good, healthy decisions and appropriate choices. Having, too, lost touch with her emotional world through gambling, she has lost the ability to tolerate intensity of emotion and so forgotten the enormous strength it can take to sit with feeling, and certainly forgotten that the ability to do this can give us enormous strength to face life and so live life well. She often equates strength with physical strength and willpower and/or believes that if we have strength it means that we will find nothing about life upsets us at all, she imagines that strong women do not feel. If, therefore, Group can be controlled and made predictable, she then lessens the likelihood that she will be taken by surprise by any unsettling thoughts and feelings that she is convinced are always destined to be her Achilles heel, rendering her vulnerable to intolerable pain and ultimately the living death of gambling addiction. Addiction puts us into a childlike state. Not trusting that she can make Adult decisions, a woman will often have a strong craving for her perception of a strong mother figure that will make those decisions for her. If strong women do not feel and they take control by force, as often she may sadly have witnessed in her life, I am frequently interpreted initially as being a weak woman for working with a warm and emotionally sensitive model. Often in the early weeks of Women's Groups I have been put under pressure to tell women what they should do, to be more directive, to take more control. I resist the temptation to 'Please others', as hard as it is at times, because I truly believe, and have seen endless evidence in Group, in the fact that for the women members they need to practise making decisions, taking appropriate levels of control, speaking up for themselves, standing up for themselves. That it is absolutely invaluable to learn that there can be a strength greater than they ever imagined possible to own in being able to tolerate a level of uncertainty about what will happen next, to witness that strength does not necessarily equate with physical strength or a 'tough love' approach that they might have experienced in some schools of addiction treatment. This all creates trust in the place we all need it most before we can truly begin to take the risk of trusting another; and that is deep within ourselves.

Not only is it of paramount importance that a member learns to trust in others who are trustworthy, but it is equally of benefit if she can begin to gain the experience of being trusted by others. Gambling is by its very nature incredibly hard to detect. There are no obvious physical symptoms as there might be with drug or alcohol addiction. This means that when eventually gambling is either disclosed by the woman with the problem or discovered by a family member or friend either by accident or through investigation due to suspicion as to where her time and money are being spent, friends and family can experience a terrifying shock and the sense of betrayal and broken trust cuts deeply and leaves a wound to their ability to trust in her in the future. After all, if they did not know that she was gambling in the first place – and perhaps for several years her gambling had remained the hidden addiction as often it has been described – then how will they know if she has relapsed? Gambling costs money; that is a fact. And if we were to analyse for any of us the meaning of money we would not have to work at great depth before we would uncover associations with stability and security if we have enough money, and the feeling that life is unstable and insecure if we do not. Friends and family therefore are understandably scared and suspicious that the woman's gambling addiction has the power to shake the very foundations of their lives. Out of this fear that her addiction could suck dry their financial resources and send financial life spinning out of control, they sometimes will try to redress the balance and counterbalance their fear of feeling out of control by taking control of finances to an inappropriate and unhelpful level. A few months' 'money management' with the agreement of the woman who has the gambling problem can indeed be very helpful and enable her to let go of the pressure to worry about money, and the battle of her inner conflict with the part of her that does not want to gamble ever again fearing that the battle will be won by the part of her that still craves the escape, the self-soothing, the altered consciousness, the lift of mood, the hope that it offers. Too tight a control on her finances and long-term questioning of her intentions, her behaviour, her trustworthiness can produce the very result that the fearful family members or friends have been desperate to avoid. She feels no benefits to putting in the day-by-day and sometimes hour-by-hour hard work of remaining gambling free; she is given no room to move. It is, after all, only actions with which she can prove that she has genuinely changed this time. Lacking autonomy, lacking a sense of empowerment, choice and freedom, all of the elements that combine to allow us to feel an adult self in the world, she feels trapped. She feels essentially the psychological and emotional triggers to her gambling in the first place. And so, left to go on, relapse occurs, triggered by all the same 'Please others', 'Work hard', 'Don't tell' rules that drove her to it in the first place.

The woman herself is plagued by a constant guilt that eats away at the delicate flesh of her self-esteem and she often will talk of understanding fully why she does not deserve to be trusted by those close to her; that she has lied and manipulated to get money to get her fix, to cover her debts, to cover her tracks when there have been questions about lost time. Often my role in Group, as previously discussed, is to give her permission *not* to feel this constant, crippling guilt through understanding *why* she was so desperate to gamble that she behaved in the way that she did, which now disgusts her. Often she is desperate to prove to herself and to others that she is so much more than the selfish, self-obsessed, money-obsessed and greedy woman that she saw when looking at the reflection of herself in the distorting mirror of gambling addiction. To be able to peel off and throw away that label of 'gambler'. The chance to prove herself is essential to recovery; without that chance she feels she cannot move on, she is forever labelled as untrustworthy, a liar and manipulative. She might as well be hanged for a sheep as a lamb, why would she not be tempted to gamble if all around her constantly suspect and treat her as though she has? Women's Group allows that chance, the chance to be in a group of others who know all the tricks, who have lied and manipulated, in desperation. Often the underlying motivation for their addiction being that somewhere along the path of life their trust in others has been shattered. And yet each woman is willing to begin to try to put the pieces back together and to begin to trust again. In a group full of women who are gamblers, she may have the first experience in many years and in many relationships of being seen as the woman that she truly is underneath the set of behaviours of which she is so deeply ashamed, that had become the necessary tool kit for accessing her addiction. This will help build a sense of self-worth, of being of value to others, to her Women's Group, to her family, to her friends and to wider society. Let us now join Women's Group at week nine and see how already trust is beginning to take its place in this group.

Things had moved on from our plate of biscuits and jug of water on the coffee table. Refreshments had been revised and become an option also of tea and coffee at the general consensus of a group discussion about whether it might be good to have hot drinks available as the weather was now into winter. Paula had brought in a spare kettle and Helen had taken up the role of 'drinks monitor', asking everyone what they wanted to drink as they entered the room and before check in began. Helen seemed to enjoy this role and the other women equally to enjoy being taken care of and asked what they would like to drink. I notice that Terri again refuses a drink and takes out her bottle of water, which each week she brings with her, in that way excluding herself from what is a sense of collaboration and ritual to this three-week old development to the start of Group. I take my seat and listen and watch as everyone settles in, usually with light conversation topics discussed, such as current soap opera story lines or comments about children or other family members. I am aware as I am each week now that the Group members have been engaging in conversation about deeper topics whilst waiting in reception area, or possibly even on the way to the station after last week's Group and wonder whether these issues will be raised in Group today. I am aware too as is now a pattern for Women's Groups that as the group grows closer together, my role in it becomes increasingly unique, in that I am a part of Women's Group, but not quite a part of it. I feel a little regret for the fact that I cannot truly join in and share my week and amusing stories with these women I am getting to know so well and developing attachments to.

As trust and attachments between Group members grow and I move from being perhaps a key attachment figure for women, as the familiar figure, the professional who might be trusted to maintain at least the boundaries of her profession, when she cannot predict reactions of the other women, to being the therapist who is not quite the same as, but not entirely different either, by nature of the fact that I am a woman and that I demonstrate understanding of the dynamics of gambling addiction.

> *On the surface it would seem that Terri craved both a sense of belonging and to be a part of things, but that simultaneously, she rejected them. At check in, she had developed a pattern of ensuring that she checked in last and then would take at least 10 to 15 minutes to do so. I was aware that this week she seemed to be engineering this situation again and I wondered how it would be received by the rest of Group, as I had been observing that it was causing some irritation in Sarah and Janet, who had not voiced their feelings, but their facial expressions and tense body language had spoken what their words had not.*

I had made a conscious decision not to intervene at that stage over the amount of time that Terri was taking to check in. At the beginning of each Group I suggest that check in is a couple of minutes and so all were aware of this guideline. I have learned that there is more for each woman to learn about how good she is at getting her own needs met, standing up for herself, protecting her won space and getting her own voice heard if I watch and wait and see how Group will manage such situations. Just as with the issue of refreshments, it is interesting for everyone to reflect on their own process; are they someone who falls quickly into 'Please others' by wanting to cater for the other Group members, symbolically perhaps putting their own needs aside to meet those of others first, as they do in life outside. Or are they someone who tends to say 'I don't mind' when asked what they want, or wait to see what everyone else is having before they commit themselves to tea or coffee? This is symbolic perhaps of not wishing to take the risk of rejection by having needs and wants or by being different? Or that they never have been afforded time and space to listen to the inner voice that actually always does know what we want and need if we take the time to tune into it and turn down the volume of the recording that says 'Don't think' or 'Don't be important'. There is the same value in my not jumping in to rescue the situation too soon, so each Group member might learn how they react or respond when they feel one member is eating up an unfair amount of time for themselves.

> *Sarah was checking in and once again, as in every meeting so far, she was weeping as she described her situation at home. She was*

frustrated and angry with her husband, whom she felt was abusing his position of power over the family finances. She had managed a couple of weeks free from gambling, but his refusal to allow her any money to do anything outside of the family home unaccompanied by him or her sons was leaving her feeling infantilised, and these feeling we had identified as triggers for potential relapse to gambling for escape from feelings about the situation, just as she had literally escaped from her controlling parents at the age of 15. It was becoming apparent to Sarah that she had been feeling trapped by the tightening confines of her marriage and role as a carer since her husband became ill and that gambling had perhaps been a way of removing herself psychologically and emotionally from the situation whilst remaining a physical presence for her family. In that way she had done a deal with herself; the deal was that she would stay and practically care for her husband and so ease her guilty feelings at wanting to be free and wanting more for herself. Even after just two weeks free of gambling it was harder for her to pretend to herself that she was happy with her life at home. Sarah seemed as always very aware of the time that she had taken up – although well within five minutes – and seemed keen to hand check in over to Terri.

Terri told us of her daughters, and the closeness with them, which she valued. She then said that she had not experienced that closeness anywhere, with anyone else and that she had been thinking of leaving Women's Group because she felt the odd one out, and that she was not wanted. Suddenly, Helen said 'I want to ask you something. Why is it that you never have a drink? I'm not being funny, but you say that you always feel the odd one out, but you don't join in'. Terri seemed shocked by having been seen in this way and I noticed that Janet's face wore what I imagined from my experience of her to be an expression of anger. While Terri was still thinking of a response, Janet added 'Maybe because you don't want to join in? I don't think you join in at check in either. You say a lot, but you don't tell us anything. Not really. All you talk about is your family. I know your daughters better than I know you'. I noticed that there were nods of agreement from around the group circle and I wondered how Terri was feeling to be the subject of a rare thing; a confrontation by the whole group to one individual. Terri became angry and said that this was evidence of exactly what she had thought, that she was not wanted there in Women's Group and that they thought she did not fit in and that she was going to get her things together and leave immediately. She looked at me and apologised for the fact that she *had to leave. I responded that of course she was free to leave if she chose, but that I hoped she would not. That I could understand her feeling very hurt and upset if she felt that she was not wanted and the odd one out, but that although she felt that way, perhaps she might stay a moment to think about whether or not it was actually true. I went on to say that I remembered that one thing which she had told us was that she had never felt wanted by her own mother and that it must be very hard indeed to believe that anyone else might want her if her own mother did not. I also said that perhaps if because of that she was always anticipating rejection it felt safer not to join in, in the first place? Even in the smaller ways like sharing refreshments? Terri looked tearful as I finished speaking and I let her sit with her thoughts and feelings for a moment. I then looked at both Helen and Janet and asked them to clarify whether what I had heard was right, that what they were saying in the subtext of their telling Terri that she did not join in was that they wanted her to be closer, to become a part of Women's Group. They wanted to get to know her better. They both agreed that this was so, that they did not want her to leave, but wanted her to truly join and to take part. Paula then said that she wanted to say that she was sorry if she had made Terri feel unwanted, too. It transpired that Terri had asked for Paula's phone number and had then tried to telephone Paula on a few occasions. Paula had answered once or twice but then began to feel overwhelmed by the frequent and lengthy telephone calls and so stopped answering her phone to Terri. Terri was silently weeping now. She then said that this happened to her all the time, that people tell her she is 'too much' and then reject her. That it made her feel that there was no value to her apart from in her identity as mother.*

We saw in action Paula's response to Terri's frequent calls and Group's response to her clinging on to every moment of attention during check in and yet still living by 'Don't be close' by staying stuck in safe, practical talk and rejecting the refreshments. Like a child that is denied what it wants in an attempt to protect its feelings will sometimes say that it never wanted it anyway, Terri had learned to pretend that she did not want to be close, as a result of the abuse by her mother and her father's allowing of it, she believed was of no value in relationship to anyone and so had lived her life by the rules of 'Don't belong' and 'Don't be close' as a form of self-protection. In her role as mother she was able safely to get the intimacy that she had the right to expect from her parents but had been denied. She still found it hard to be close with others outside of the family and if she did allow herself to become close she became anxiously attached (Bowlby, 1986), constantly fearing and predicting the rejection she was convinced would come, and eventually bringing it about because she would cling so hard to the other that they would feel suffocated and reject her. This would leave her more convinced than ever that she was unlovable and that it was safer to live life by 'Don't be close'. As her daughters were growing and developing lives of their own, Terri began to experience loneliness and was isolated outside of her work and relationship with her husband. Gambling, we were to discover as Women's Group process moved on, had been a way of her shutting off from her lonely feelings and at times too from flashbacks from her childhood abuse, which began troubling her now that her daughters allowed her less time to focus on their needs.

What we have seen in the response of Women's Group is a phenomenon that I have witnessed consistently in every Women's Group I have facilitated. That is, that there is rarely anything that a woman can say in terms of describing shameful things that she has done which will provoke feelings of anger and mistrust by Group as a whole. It is what she does *not* say that is much more likely to do so. Uncertainty is a theme along with certain others that always triggers fear in Women's Group. It is frequently discussed in Group as one of the most difficult states to tolerate and is often a trigger for gambling in an attempt to control the anxiety attached to it. I have witnessed before that if a Group member is assumed to be consistently hiding in Group, then the collective fear this engenders tends to provoke a 'fight' response to fear (Bradford Cannon, 1915). This is unusual as individually the women in the early stages of group therapy find expressing anger extremely difficult. Perhaps it is the feeling of safety in numbers; perhaps it is the instinctive desire to protect the other Group members that enables anger to manifest and confrontation to occur. I have noticed too that Group members and Group as a whole present a very different response that of a woman who is quiet because of shyness or shame and embarrassment, or mental health problems, and will conversely respond in a way that is understanding, encouraging and nurturing towards the woman concerned. It is the perceived withholding for reasons that they do not understand; again we return to uncertainty that triggers such a dramatic fear response.

Although to have confrontation and conflict in Women's Group in this early stage is quite rare, it does not have to be disastrous. The important thing always is to encourage the women involved to stay in the room and work to identify what the real issues are, individually and collectively, and to resolve them. This can be a massive step forward in the recovery process in itself as most women will have learned that there is a danger in dealing head on with conflict and confrontation and be very fearful of the consequences, and so their default mode has invariably been to run to the relative safety of gambling to attempt to block out their upset and anger. Any attempt to run from the group room is an opportunity for the Group member to learn what it is that triggers her gambling. What are the situational, emotional and psychological triggers? We see them there in Women's Group *in action*. And she has a chance to do something different, not to run but to stand and face the fears that have stalked her for so long. In conflict resolution too, she has the opportunity to learn the valuable lesson that:

Falling out does not have to mean falling apart.

To women such as Terri and the other members of her Women's Group they have perhaps never before had that experience. Falling out has meant blame and accusations that are never resolved, destruction of important relationship, and sadly of yet another part of their already cracked and fading self-worth. In the worst cases it has meant the channelling of another's angry feelings into abusive actions, which they have experienced or witnessed. It has meant their channelling into gambling addiction their own sadness, anger, guilt and the depression and anxiety resulting from the loneliness of living by 'Don't belong' and 'Don't be close'.

Through this Women's Group meeting we have begun to see that there are particular themes that thread themselves through each Women's Group I have facilitated since 2007. Let us take some time to highlight these themes and how they each interplay with the addiction to gambling that each woman enters group therapy to confront.

Anger

Women who attend Women's Group for problem gambling almost always use gambling to suppress angry feelings. Gambling may and frequently does serve several purposes for the Group member but I have found the suppression of anger always to be one of them. At some point in life she has experienced or witnessed anger used inappropriately or abusively by another and has made a decision that it is not safe to feel angry. If she is driven to 'Please others' she may have learned that being angry does not fit with this drive, that others certainly are not pleased and that perhaps bad things happen as a consequence. She may, too, fear the consequences of the power of her own anger. For all of us, if we constantly suppress our anger, the pressure of containing it tends to bring it simmering ever nearer to boiling point and when we do then express it, it tends to be in involuntary lid-flying-off-the-pressure-cooker explosion. We tend then not to be taken seriously in what we say or do in those moments, leaving us believing that there is no point in expressing anger, nobody listens anyway and tells us we are just being overly emotional. The woman may have found that the force of her anger in those moments has scared another. She might well have scared herself. I have heard women speak of the terror they feel at the thought of contacting the full force of their anger. I have heard stories of volcanic explosions, of the physical attack of another's property, of the fear that they are capable in those raging moments of the physical, emotional destruction of another. Of fear that I would be afraid of her was she to unleash in Women's Group the ferocity that she runs from. Gambling helps her to hide from her anger and yet does not help it to dissipate; it is still there, growing bigger in the darkness she hides it in. Women's Group, if it is working well, will allow it to surface. Sooner or later someone or something will trigger her anger and she can began to learn that in acknowledging its existence she gains control over it, she can begin to manage it by expressing moment by moment the little niggles when they arise rather than stuffing them down with gambling where they grow wild and uncontrollable. She can learn the difference between anger and aggression and how to be appropriately assertive.

Attachment

What every woman I have met in Women's Group most wants and yet at the same time what she most fears. With so many stories shared of destructive relationship and damaged attachments in childhood, it is perhaps sadly of no surprise that this should be so. Again, this fear of what is one of our most essential needs is one of the primary reasons that it is so hard to encourage women into treatment for problem gambling either in one-to-one or especially in group therapy. Here, there are so many more people to get close to for comfort and pleasure and support and all that it is to be joyfully human, but also to fear another round of hurt and pain. It is this hurt and pain that the Group member has been hiding from in gambling. Just like Terri, women find if they do manage to allow themselves to get close it tends to be an anxious attachment (Bowlby, 1986). Again, just as Terri found, to live a life by 'Don't be close' leads to loneliness and depression and the anxiety we feel when we have little or no 'back up' in life. Gambling addiction can numb us to loneliness and lift for a moment a depression it has caused, or stop for a time the rapidly spiralling, crazy-making anxious thoughts. It is however, a cold companion. For the woman who can tolerate her fears of being close and attaching long enough to develop an attachment to her Group she soon begins to experience the difference in being close with others who can fully witness her in all her myriad of emotions and the richness in truly intimate relationship. That sometimes living by 'Don't be close' as a self-protection mechanism is where the real danger lies. It leads to finding relationships as remote as possible where we are shielded from true human contact through a computer screen, or finding 'friends' in online bingo sites or amusement arcades where again these remote friendships come at the high price of emotional and mental health as the addiction to gambling has taken hold.

Betrayal

Betrayal and damaged trust are intrinsically linked. The majority of women whom I meet in Women's Group have had their trust betrayed by someone they were close with. Whether it is through the pain of being lied to in romantic relationship or in the extreme being abused by someone they trusted, the emotional damage has the greatest impact. This type of woman arrives in Group suspicious of further betrayal and so is guarded. Perhaps 'Don't feel' has helped her to navigate her way through the treacherous waters of close relationship so far and gambling has been a way of living life by this rule. At times when she has come close to feeling anything she deems threatening she has gambled away not just her money but her feelings until both are spent. When betrayal has been an issue for her, she has perhaps been driven by 'Be strong' and associated this with having no feelings. Feelings leave us open and vulnerable. The woman who has been hit by and still suffers from the dull ache of betrayal is likely to fear her own tears. 'I don't do crying', as Sarah said. We feel very vulnerable when we weep. What I have been taught throughout my specialisation of women and gambling is that, regardless of any pain that she may have suffered from treatment by a man she is close with, if there has been betrayal by a woman she is close with the wound penetrates a level deeper. There appears to be something deeply damaging and shocking about betrayal by one's own sex. This has profound effects on her all round wellbeing, as her lack of trust in women then leaves her cut off from the support and all round health benefits of spending time with her own sex. Janet shared with us how difficult it was for her to be in a group of women, having been betrayed by her mother, who broke her promise and abandoned her. The invaluable role of Women's Group with this issue is of course in providing a safe space where a member might experience that not all women need to be kept locked out of her life. She can see in action how she tends to transfer all her negative associations with women she has known who have betrayed her onto new women she encounters. She can practise developing flexible boundaries and being more discerning about whom she might trust to let in.

Disappointment (fear of)

So many women I have worked with over the years cut themselves off from looking forward in life, at least with any degree of optimism, for fear of the crushing blow dealt to them by disappointment. Life has taught them that there will always be an intolerable low to follow any high, or even any time of contentment, and if they do reach a plateau they are suspicious of the hole in the ground they imagine is about to open up and drag them back down into the depths. Not looking forward to anything is a way of attempting to exercise some control over feelings and emotions. If we do not look forward, we avoid the pain and sadness of disappointment. So too do we avoid the sparkle of having things to look forward to. Fear of disappointment can block us from making life adjustments or improvements. What is the point if we imagine that we will always be disappointed and that what we build must always be destroyed? If we fear disappointment, what we do allow ourselves to build is a safe house where we can hide from all that we perceive risks our feelings being crushed and we stay hidden there. Gambling addiction has often been a perceived safe house to hide in; nothing will change, little will get better while the gambling is so out of control that it controls all aspects of one's life. The consequences of gambling, the wins followed by the lows and anxieties of loss only compound the belief that something bad always happens. Women's Group can help a member to identify this pattern of negative thinking and behaving that she has become frozen by. It can help her to understand that, to an extent, she is right and that, yes, life will always bring along ups and downs and disappointments; she experiences in the moment, in Group, that, yes too, if we become close to others it is likely that at some point, to some extent, they will let us down and disappoint us. The art of life is not allowing it to destroy us or our hope for the future, so that we go with the flow of life and do not become frozen for fear of feeling disappointed. This is essential to recovery as she must allow herself to build on the barren landscape of her life that will be left when space is cleared that has been taken up by gambling and after it is gone, the mess it has left behind.

Guilt and shame

The consequences of gambling behaviour are devastating to life and relationship. Debts, relationships in tatters, the woman affected by gambling has behaved in ways that leave her racked with guilt and unrecognisable to herself when she measures the way that she behaved when caught in addiction and consumed by cravings to gamble by her values and morals when she has removed herself from the trap that was her addiction. Her guilt can leave her feeling that she is not deserving of anything good in life; that she must make amends by denying herself any time and any financial reward as her gambling behaviour led to her wasting unaffordable amounts of both time and money. It adds fuel to the fire that drives the engine of 'Please others' and can soon leave her spent as she tries to overcompensate for that which she feels she is guilty of and so deserves punishment for. Often I see the results of this as leading to relapse. Remove gambling from her life and life feels empty and stark, as does her inner world without the distraction of her addiction. It is vital that she allows herself to spend time doing the things that might ultimately be rewarding and that she allows herself, too, to be financially as comfortable as is possible. Too tight a rein on finances can provoke gambling urges as a way of maybe winning a little money, or of lifting a low mood caused by a dull, empty life and no money to make a few healthy choices here and there, as we heard when Sarah described her early recovery struggles. In Women's Group I see women encourage each other by reflecting their understanding of why gambling took hold for the woman they are hearing share her story. They assure her she is valuable and that she is worth spending time and money on. Their words are not empty because they are backed up by how they have experienced that woman in Group, that she has perhaps been a source of strength and support for another member, or that they admire the way she speaks of her love for her family.

Loss

The fear of loss is deep within many of the women who attend Women's Groups. The moment we have something that we value, to an extent are we not all afraid of losing it? The loss of relationship is something that most of the women I work with are fearful of. Perhaps they have experienced the pain of loss through abandonment, as had Janet, or loss through bereavement; they know the grief of losing someone that they cared for and were close to. In many cases feelings are unresolved and have been locked tightly away in a box for fear of the intensity of grief they will evoke and that the feelings may never abate. Gambling has been a way of locking the lid down tightly if the contents start to spill out. For fear of further pain they have retreated into 'Don't be close', 'Be strong', 'Don't feel'. When these rules have failed to protect them from feeling or when the loneliness they invited becomes overwhelming they have used gambling as a salve for their feelings. Recovery from gambling addiction will require grieving for a loss; the loss of gambling. Losing what they partly want will cause a grieving process that is similar to the loss of a relationship with a loved one. With all of the denial, anger and depression to work through before they reach the freedom of acceptance. In Women's Group, they will not have to go through this painful process alone. One of the benefits of Group being open-ended is that often there are members who are a few steps ahead in the recovery process and can sit by a new member's side when she becomes stuck for a while and needs to rest before moving on, or can encourage her if she falls back or doubts herself, as they have been down the same path and know that each phase of the grieving process will pass. They now know too, from their own experience of Women's Group that it is so much easier with support.

Regret

Regret is a sense of disappointment but, in a woman affected by gambling's case, this time with herself. Her gambling-free self in recovery looks back at herself imprisoned by gambling, just as someone might, having served a lengthy prison sentence, have a chasm of regret for the things that she did do and the things that she did not do because she was preoccupied with her gambling addiction. In Women's Group we see women grieving and full of remorse for wasted money in amounts so great that stable homes could have been bought. Far greater however, than any regret for any amount of money wasted, is the overwhelming grief for wasted time and wasted lives. Grief for the person she might have been, the way her relationships might have been, for the fact that children have grown before her very eyes but she has not truly seen them growing up, as gambling addiction has stood in the way and blocked her view. As one woman in a previous Group said, 'We can always make more money, but we cannot make more time'. In Women's Group she has the opportunity to share her regret and the accompanying grief. As her trust builds she may feel more confidence in sharing what are often shameful experiences that are linked with regret as she senses that these women who have also been frozen by gambling addiction will understand and empathise. Her regret for time and chances lost, once she has reached a place of acceptance, are then often seen transformed into a healthy and stalwart resolution to waste no more time and to invest in herself and life; to spend whatever time she has wisely.

Rejection

For many women rejection is a familiar feeling, and yet the sickening pain that crushes and grinds their self-worth to an even lower level is not eased by the repetition. Perhaps, as for Terri, the Group member has now come to expect it and attempts to avoid the feelings by either clinging on tightly and anxiously to the person she is close to or, conversely, by avoiding closeness at all costs. If she is close to nobody, then nobody is likely to see whom she truly is. The self that she has become as a result of her gambling addiction, she believes is unacceptable to others, especially so before she has reached any level of self-acceptance. Fear of rejection from Women's Group manifests itself sometimes in silence too, or in moments when a woman might rip off her mask to reveal what she believes to be the horror beneath, rather than sitting waiting for rejection, risking getting close only to be rejected when Group knows who she *really* is; she feels in control if she brings on the rejection. One woman attempted just this, describing herself in her first ever Women's Group check in: 'I know what I am, I'm a liar, I'm a thief, I'm a cheat. I am *scum*'. It did not work. Women's Group did not reject her, as had her three sisters, when they discovered her gambling addiction. Women's Group saw through her words and saw what she was attempting to do, because so many women know that trick oh so well. 'Get them to reject me' is better than sitting and waiting for it to happen. Women's Group is a great place to learn to take that risk.

Separation

We see often in Group meetings that separation brings with it anxieties. We see later in this book that therapist illness or holidays, or the unexplained or regular absence of a Group member provokes fears of permanent loss or rejection. Sometimes a Group member will wonder, was it something that she said or did in the last meeting that has driven the absent member away? This may especially be a fear if there has been a confrontation in Group, or strong feelings have been aired. We need to remember that women come to Women's Group having been used to hiding from just such things in gambling, fearing that there will be a negative consequence if they break the 'Don't be who you truly are' rule. Separation can bring with it uncertainty and all of the associated fears. In the age of instant access to each other via mobile phones and social networking, we get little practice at learning to be healthily separate and managing the uncertainty it brings. When we are in addiction we are frozen into a stasis, we are in truth a childlike self that has not developed since the addiction began because there has been no time to focus on personal growth; life has been all about satiating addictive cravings or clearing up the aftermath. Let us remember too, that the reason for so many women becoming addicted to gambling lies in histories of abuse or neglect. Again when a woman has survived these experiences as a child she will have had no time to grow into a healthy adult, all of her attention will have been on the dangerous environment, not her inner world. Physically she is a woman taking her place in Women's Group but, emotionally and psychologically, she may be still a child. As children we do not cope well with separation, we fear we will not survive if the other does not return. When self-worth is at an all-time low and a woman values herself so little, it is hard to believe that the other will bear her in mind, that she is worthy of the other wanting to return to her.

Trust

Trust is ever a piece of the puzzle we fit together in Women's Group to complete the picture of why a woman's gambling problem began, where she is now, and how she will move forward into a productive, healthy and fulfilling life. If others had not broken her trust in them, if she could have trusted others for emotional and practical support, if she could trust herself to take care of herself, to make a good, healthy life and good relationship choices, she would not be in Women's Group for problem gambling because she would not have been gambling addictively. That is what my clinical experience has taught me. We need trust to have a good relationship with ourselves and with others and as I said at the very start of this book, I truly believe it is all about relationship. In essence, she is in Women's Group to learn to trust and to relate again. It sounds so simple, but I think that most women I have met in Women's Group would say it is one of the hardest tasks of all.

Uncertainty

If we are uncertain it is like we have a blank wall before us and onto that wall we can project a film of 101 scenarios that might run through our head, good or bad. Being uncertain can create anxiety, because we are not in control. We do not know whether the next hour might bring us elation, disappointment, frustration or misery, so we feel unprepared. In order to prepare ourselves we sometimes imagine the worst as we discussed earlier in this chapter. Or, perhaps we sit for hours and even days, ruminating, trying to come up with an answer, as if we had a crystal ball in our mind that, if we gaze into long enough, will give us an image of what to expect. What this tends to do in actuality is driving us to feel increasingly anxious and depressed as our thoughts whirl ever faster, seeking the needle in the haystack. For the woman who attends Women's Group this has often driven her to gamble, to escape the thoughts she feels will drive her crazy and the paralysing anxiety they evoke. Women's Group certainly will bring to a head this fear of uncertainty; from day one on the journey, as we heard from Paula, through to uncertainties around other members, the Group process, Group therapist, through to how she will feel without gambling, how she will feel at the end of Group. This, however, is one of the wonderful, if terrifying, things about Women's Group; it reverses the process of problem gambling, which is all about running to avoid. Women's Group is about the standing still and facing and learning to deal with that which scares her so much she preferred to put herself through the pain and misery of gambling addiction.

Chapter 4

Meeting halfway through the process

Let us return to Women's Group having pressed fast forward so that we are now at the six-month period. We are now in March and halfway through the life of Women's Group at a time when the world is just coming back to life after the harshness of winter. Does the context of the time of year have any significance, you might be asking? Yes, I believe that in fact it does, that the seasons do affect attendance, mood and motivation in Women's Group and in one-to-one work. Summer, in the world of gambling addiction treatment, has often seen numbers of women and men seeking treatment falling. I have often wondered if this makes sense in terms of people naturally feeling better because of the soothing effects of the sunshine, if we take it as a given that one of the ways in which gambling to excess is used is as a form of self-medication, a way of lifting low mood or soothing painful feelings. Perhaps for a time the sun, which can of course have the same effect, does not take away the gambling problem, but certainly can make the consequences seem a little less dark and so delay the need to seek help and support.

Another much more practical reason for women not approaching treatment during the summer season is of course that of childcare. For the woman who is at home with children, the long summer holidays make it difficult to put aside the time and find childcare for the hour-and-a-half Women's Group meeting plus her travel time either side. She makes a big time commitment when she commits to the Group process. It is easy to say of course that both time and childcare can always be found, but let us remember that we are dealing with addiction and that with addiction comes chaotic thinking, and so something that might seem simple enough from an outside perspective can seem 'mission impossible' to the woman who is maybe depressed and so lack of motivation makes everything seem twice as hard and take twice as long. High anxiety and preoccupation with gambling make focusing on additional planning difficult. Once into recovery these things may be a little easier from a practical point of view, but then she is facing the painful period of regret and remorse that brings to the surface guilty feelings about the time and money spent gambling rather than with and on her children. She may then find it hard to justify to herself being away from her children and fall into a pattern of over-compensation; even though rationally she may be aware that attending Women's Group is healthy for her and her recovery, everything in her that feels what it is to be 'Mother' will be in conflict with her thoughts, and this strong maternal instinct, backed up by the driving force of her guilt, will often win out. Childcare, for the many women I meet who do not have the marvellous benefits of a supportive extended family and helpful close friends, will often have a financial cost. This is an additional financial burden to bear when we are all so well aware of the devastation that gambling addiction wreaks on finances. Where money is concerned, in the world of problem gambling treatment often it can be heard said 'Well, she could find the money to gamble, why can't she find the money for childcare/travel/treatment . . . ?' It is indeed true that she could have found that same amount of money and probably quadrupled it for her gambling addiction. The problem is *where* and *how* she got that money. Cravings to gamble have led her to beg, steal, borrow, to take out payday loans she can never hope to repay, to pawn everything of monetary or even sentimental value, to go without food, all to feed her addiction. Now she has reduced or stopped gambling, money in and for the 'real world' has a very different value from 'gambling money' and she will be reluctant to and often afraid of going back to feeling anxious and vulnerable as she did when having behaved irresponsibly with money. She will struggle to spend one penny more than she can afford, even to buy something that ultimately will help her to take in the long term more responsibility for her finances and for herself as an individual member of Women's Group and in groups in wider society. Of course, again, if she is an established Women's Group member and can bring herself to come to Group, often her Women's Group will encourage her to attend regularly by feeling her guilt and doing it anyway! An important life skill, feeling guilty about an action does not necessarily indicate it is the wrong thing to do. For many women post-gambling addiction, who are mothers, if they never did anything they felt guilty about, they would never do anything at all.

Autumn, and the changing of the clocks from British Summer Time to bring in darker evenings, can herald problems not only for a drop in mood, but also for a drop in attendance for evening Group meetings as women fear travelling home alone in the dark. The Women's Group we are following is not affected by this of course as it is a morning Group, but I am aware of this as an issue if I do offer evening Women's Groups and prefer to run them no later than 6pm to 7.30pm, as many women are naturally nervous of the dark evenings, and frequently women who attend have struggled with agoraphobia and/or suffer panic attacks outside of the home. The emotional and psychological process of being in Women's Group is at times challenging enough for every woman; I therefore believe that the physical getting to and from the venue should be as easy as possible. When I spoke of this belief in a Group meeting, Helen insightfully said 'Good idea, Liz. Then it stops us using travel as an excuse to ourselves for why we can't come!'

Winter brings with it, whether we like it or not, Christmas time. What I have found over the years of Women's Group meetings is that many women who attend do *not* like it. Christmas fills shops, television screens, radio broadcasts and so too our minds with the notion of family and friends drawing together. Even for those of us with comfortable lives, friends and family there are additional pressures to 'Work hard' and 'Please others', to spend money we do not have. Let us imagine how that is for the woman who has gambled herself into a pit of debt and yet feels guilt-driven to over-compensate and to make sure that others do not miss out on gifts as a result of her taking money from where it was needed in desperation to gamble. The dark, dismal, grey reality of her money worries, her debt, her loneliness and isolation all seem magnified and held up in contrast to the gaudy tinsel and twinkling fairy lights. Memories of Christmas past along with any ghosts that haunt her return, triggered by the powerful images we are force fed at Christmas time. One woman I met and worked with in one-to-one treatment and Women's Group for two years could not see a Christmas tree without it triggering flashbacks of the sexual abuse she endured as a child, which would worsen each Christmas time when her father had been drinking. Gambling on slot machines was her way of blocking out those images, of hiding away from the Christmas lights by taking shelter in the lights of the amusement arcade.

Had we been in our Women's Group at the build up to Christmas time we would have seen and heard familiar themes of sadness and regret for the fact that families, as the Group members would like them to be, remain the Disney onscreen fantasy. For Helen it was a lonely time, estranged from most of her own family and unable to be with her partner, who went home to her parents, as her partner hid her relationship with Helen from her parents along with the fact that she was a lesbian. This left Helen feeling lonely, rejected and abandoned, but she hid these feelings from her partner, guilt leading her to feel that she did not deserve to ask her partner to spend Christmas with her, when she had caused her so much upset through her gambling addiction. Helen at this point was struggling still to gain gambling-free time beyond a few days at a time. Helen found that she had gambled every day of the separation.

Terri had found Christmas marked the growing gap in the closeness between her and her daughters as they had spent a great deal of the holiday out with their friends, leaving Terri feeling abandoned, angry with her daughters for disappointing her when she had invested as usual large amounts of both time and money in preparing in detail the family Christmas. So strong was her identity as mother and so weak was her sense of self as Terri that she had returned to Women's Group contemplating trying to having another baby.

The strong desire to have another child when an existing child becomes an independent adult is something women frequently speak of in Women's Group and in one-to-one therapy. Many women who have been blessed never to have known the trap of addiction experience this longing to hold onto their maternal role when children are flying the nest, of course. The change means reassessing one's role as a mother, as the need of the woman to be needed is no longer met in the same way. If the woman has had little life outside of home and family, this change can seem like a daunting prospect. For the woman who has a gambling addiction, she faces these same issues. Her identity is likely to be even less defined outside that of the mother role because her addiction to gambling will not only have swallowed up her thoughts and feelings about the things she could not bear to be aware of but also swallowed whole her sense of self. She has had no time to grow and develop a strong sense of what she likes and dislikes, what her interests and passions are, how she likes to spend her time, and with whom. Her addiction and its consequences will have preoccupied her, and with the little time she did have left she would have been focused on being 'mother' and, often driven by the guilt and shame caused by her gambling, over-compensated by 'over-parenting'. The same guilt and shame would have caused her to cut herself off from others and so to depend more on her children as her only source of human contact, the only trusted source of emotional intimacy. This is especially so for those many women who have issues of abuse at the root of their addiction. To have another child – no matter how much genuinely loved – would be often subconsciously an attempt to lose themselves once again in the world of motherhood, just as they lost themselves in the world of gambling. Again, there would be no time and space to think about who they are outside of this world of motherhood, or to take the risk of going out into the world and fully engaging with it. It also can feel like a second chance, a chance to put right all that they regret, a salve to the sadness they feel for the time lost to gambling and so lost to time spent with their children. The new life would perhaps be a way of her avoiding grieving for their loss, for not only the loss of their mother role, but all that was lost whilst they were so closely intertwined in their relationships with gambling.

Paula had returned home to visit her family, but this was a troubling and distressing visit as family brought back memories of the sexual abuse she had suffered throughout childhood. She had struggled with the uncertainty of whether the now elderly uncle who had abused her would be present at the family gathering. She felt betrayed by her sisters, who had invited him, despite knowing that he had abused Paula. She had bought some scratch cards both during and after the family visit. Scratch cards give a realistic chance of winning a large enough sum of money to be, for her, life changing. When Paula was left feeling disempowered, and therefore childlike, by feeling her sisters' inconsiderate actions, making it difficult for her to set firm boundaries over which her uncle could not cross, the hope of a win was both a distraction and the chance of a windfall that she thought would have given her some of the choice, power and freedom associated with money.

For Janet, Christmas had brought for her guilt, remorse and regret for her past addictive behaviour that had led to her being separated from her children at this time for family. Although she had remained gambling-free, she had become very depressed, taking solace by absorbing herself in her church and constant prayer as God the father was a constant presence for her, unlike the birth father she had never known, or her mother or the fathers of her own children, who had abandoned her. Thinking of these betrayals and there being no Group meetings for two weeks had caused her trust in human relationships to waver once more and Janet struggled to return to Women's Group for the first two meetings following the Christmas break.

Sarah's lonely feelings were not caused by the lack of physical presence of others, yet these feelings were still very much alive for her. She felt lonely and isolated because it was becoming clearer to her that to her husband and sons she was 'wife' and 'mother' and they could not recognise her or even acknowledge her in the shape of herself as Sarah, the individual with wants and needs that might be separate from those of the family as a collective. She had been upset and angered by her husband and sons buying her an expensive vacuum cleaner as a Christmas gift, she felt this represented their image of her as a woman who was there exclusively to take care of them and the home and to remain in the home. Christmas had been a time of a full home with visits from extended family and her frail mother coming to stay. Sarah's anger and frustration at others and at herself for being caught by the drive to 'Please others' had triggered a relapse to gambling online, once again to escape while remaining a physical presence.

Having caught up with where each woman within Women's Group was within her individual process at the highly emotive time of Christmas, let us now return to take our places in Group three months after that time. Halfway into the life of Women's Group is a time of rich and constant relationship growth as each woman has developed not only in terms of how she relates with others in Women Groups, but is using what is mirrored back to her through her relationships in Group to reflect on herself and her inner world of thoughts and feelings. She understands more and more that the way she perceives and relates to the other women she meets with each week has been influenced by the way she has been treated by others she has been close to in her life. She understands too how these patterns play out in relationships outside of Women's Group and how this has influenced her gambling patterns.

At this meeting I was prepared for there to be some absent members. The week before, I had cancelled Women's Group meeting as I had been too ill to attend. Experience had taught me that it is one thing for Group to rationally understand that I am human and so I will become ill at times, but what they feel about it might be quite another matter. The more important Women's Group becomes as attachments grow, the more impact it has if a meeting has to be missed, for it means that members will miss those they are growing close to, me included. For some women who are particularly isolated and lonely, Women's Group might be one of the only events of the strikingly empty page of their calendar. They are building their confidence in building social contact and so missed meetings can be damaging to this process. For women in early recovery, the week-to-week stepping stones of Group meetings help them to step steadily along the rocky path, the aim to just get to next week's meeting without gambling. The weekly meeting is a place to replenish their resolve and by this stage of in-depth Group work, to truly experience with a conscious awareness the benefits of expressing feelings with others, rather than suppressing them with gambling. I am constantly aware that if I cancel a meeting I am disappointing each woman who was expecting to attend and that I might expect to experience many different reactions to this, some verbally communicated to me and sometimes communicated in more indirect ways such as staying away from the next meeting, their behaviour voicing their anger, or saying that trust in me has been chipped by my unpredictable behaviour in cancelling the Group meeting.

Everyone except Terri was at the meeting. She had not communicated with me to let me know that she would not be there and, as she was usually early, her absence was noticed straight away. I apologised for my absence the previous week and suggested that everyone include in their check in any thoughts and feelings they might have about that meeting being cancelled. Janet said that she understood I was ill, but that she was disappointed the meeting had to be cancelled and that as a result she had had a difficult week and struggled with gambling urges. I asked her what it was that had been missing from her life without the Group meeting and she instantly knew that it was the sense of family that she now felt in Group. She said that in the Anonymous meetings that she attended it was not the same and that although she had found this group scary at first, she now valued talking about life and exploring the reasons for gambling, rather than just talking about gambling behaviour itself. I asked her whether she had been disappointed in me and she replied that yes, she had a little, but these things happen. I felt encouraged that Janet was able to express what might be perceived as negative feelings towards me. As we have touched on before, Women's Group is a safe space for each woman to practise being her authentic self.

Paula expressed her concern for Terri and that she had not contacted me or anyone else to explain her absence, and Helen reflected her concern. Sarah looked thoughtful during this conversation and then added that something 'did not feel right' for her with Terri, that she still felt that Terri was hiding something and that she felt bad saying it, but she did not entirely believe some of the things that Terri said. Paula said that she felt the same. I asked what it felt like if they both believed that Terri was hiding and they both spoke of feeling uncomfortable, that it did not feel right because everyone else was allowing themselves to be vulnerable, which was hard work and that feeling that Terri still held back made them feel watched and judged by her. I asked what had stopped either of them from saying this to Terri herself, when there were such strong feelings around this issue. Sarah said that she did not want to upset Terri and drive a wedge between them. I asked Sarah to reflect on how she felt things might be between her and Terri in one month's time if she still felt the same and yet had said nothing to her about her feelings. Sarah thought for a few moments and said, probably things would be worse

> and that she would distance herself from Terri and be reluctant to disclose anything in front of her. That the wedge she was afraid of driving between them would become a reality. I reflected on how often that it is the case that it is the things that we choose not to say that create more problems than the things we choose to say. I said too, that I wondered how everyone thought Terri might feel if she knew that she was being discussed whilst she was not there. Paula said that she imagined it would be upsetting for her. I said that I was aware that their aim had been not to drive a wedge or to upset Terri by discussing their issues about her with her, and yet it seemed, if I was hearing right, that they thought they might bring these things about by hiding their thoughts and feelings from her. That, in a way, perhaps they were doing just the same thing that they felt Terri was doing, and hiding the truth? That their reason seemed to be out of fear of something bad happening if they confronted it. I strongly encouraged them to think about discussing these things with Terri in the next meeting.

It will sometimes happen that Group will discuss concerns they have about another member in their absence. It is a way of venting difficult thoughts and feelings and getting validation from other Group members, but avoiding the risk of conflict with the Group member they are concerned with. I have found the most valuable way to work with such situations is to use Socratic questioning to test out the theory that this will work as a strategy to avoid what is most feared – confrontation, conflict and upset, or will it in fact bring it about?

> Paula then said that she could understand why Terri might feel it was difficult to be open. That she still found it hard to be completely open in Women's Group and for her it was all about fearing she might not be believed. She shared that when she was around 11 years old she had found the courage to tell her mother that her uncle was abusing her and that she had been told not to be so silly and to go and get her school uniform ready. Paula looked upset and angry as she shared this with us. She said that to her after that there seemed no point in sharing anything with anyone; it felt easier just to block it all out. That was when she had started to self-harm, as she swapped her seemingly endless emotional pain for the physical pain that was a distraction from it. Later, she began to gamble, the focus offered by fixation on the computer screen a less physically harmful option to manage that same pain. The pain of the abuse and the pain of her

voice pleading for help being ignored, being left alone to suffer. It felt safe to hide after that rather than to take the risk of asking for help, only to be rejected again.

Sarah cried silently as she listened to Paula and spoke of how sad she felt for her. Paula said to Sarah that she was sorry for upsetting her and Sarah replied that she should not be sorry, that she was sad but happy that Paula had been able to tell us in Group what had happened and that she thought it very brave of her. Paula looked across the room at me and I shared that I too felt sad to think of the little girl that Paula had been feeling so alone with her pain and her voice not being heard.

Helen said that there was something that had happened to her which she was thinking she maybe should tell us. She said that she was worried about doing so, because any time that she had tried to talk about it she felt worse and that she became so upset and anxious that her gambling got worse and emotionally she feared it might lead to a complete breakdown. But, the more she listened to other women in Group sharing their stories, the more she understood that it was perhaps the things that caused the most pain in life that triggered gambling. That she had never really understood that until now, but suddenly, as she put it, 'the penny had dropped'. I was aware from my knowledge of Helen through our initial assessment that she was likely to be referring to the rape she experienced, but of course I would not reveal or allude to this without her clearly saying she was ready to bring this issue into the room. I turned to Helen and said that often it was the case that if there were things in life that felt too scary to talk about when they happened, then we freeze our thoughts and feelings and store them away to protect ourselves. Then, at times when we do remember what happened to us, the feelings defrost and are as strong and as fresh and as scary as when the terrible event happened. But, just as she was wondering, most people find that slowly but surely facing what happened and talking it through, although never erasing the memories, can make them less scary and the need to gamble them away is lessened too. I added that lots of women find that it is good and helpful to make sure that they have extra support in place and a plan for how to manage the fearful thoughts and feelings when they do arise and until things settle.

Offering an educational element to Women's Group is of huge value. Women come to Group often having little understanding of their inner world of thoughts and feelings, let alone where on earth gambling addiction fits with it all. To offer insight as to the basic psychology of what it is for us to be human can normalise what feels to the gambling-affected woman to be behaviour peculiar to her, and to give her a sense of belonging to a wider group still, that of being a woman, that of being human, encouraging a sense of belonging in a wider social group than a group of women who gamble. There is sometimes a strong re-parenting (Clarkson, 2003) element to my role as Women's Group therapist as many women I meet with have not had it explained to them by mothers in touch with their instinctive feminine self that it is natural to feel emotional pain, to feel fear, to be anxious. That what makes the difference between those of us who manage life and its traumas perhaps a little better than others is the relationships we have with ourselves and with others and how we process and express our uncomfortable feelings, our distress and how we self-soothe and take a little healthy escapism here and there. Like an okay parent (Berne, 2010), I attempt to offer information and education and to encourage, but not to drag and not to push women in a particular direction. Too soon a challenge to Helen to disclose, for example, could result in her going deeper underground with what she fears to reveal. Often, to talk about how it might be to disclose new material, and to put a plan in place for what to do if it raises thoughts and feelings that are difficult to tolerate, are all that is needed to give a woman courage to move forward. What we see in action above is women learning those skills from each other, we see the power of having our pain seen and heard and that those who witness it do not reject us for our feelings being too much to bear. We see the beginnings of the women in this developing Group learning to sit with and to tolerate pain, their own and that of another, even if they cannot 'fade it or fix it' (Mountain Dreamer, 2006). Such are the skills that they will need if they are not to constantly crave the always open arms of gambling addiction, which kills their pain but also in time the will to live, ultimately squeezing the joy of and will for life from them.

> *One piece of news that I had to deliver was that of a new member joining Women's Group on the following week. I had forgotten to mention this at the start of the Group meeting, before check in, as I would usually, in order to allow as much time as possible for discussion of how everyone feels about this. I apologised for my error and asked everyone to include their reflections on a new member joining us as they checked out. Everyone spoke in various ways of their being open to the experience of a new person, saying that they only hoped that she would feel comfortable and that they remembered*

what it was like at their very first meeting and how anxious they felt. Paula acknowledged the importance of growing attachments as she said that she imagined it would feel much easier for them to meet a new person than for the new woman to meet them, as they already knew each other. Helen said with a return to her infectious, exuberant humour that it would be nice to be like the big girls at school with a new girl joining. I wondered if she was using her humour to lift the mood in Group as we had been working in such depth and as everyone laughed, and I easily smiled along with them, I reflected to Group that perhaps it felt good for us to lighten the mood as we had worked very hard that day.

Let us now move forward one week to our next meeting. Once more an empty chair marked the absence of Terri. She had sent a text to apologise for not attending last week and to say that she had a dentist appointment this week, which meant once more she could not attend. I had replied to say that I was sorry we would not see her, that she would be missed and I hoped to see her next week. As with every meeting I started by welcoming everyone, and included a special welcome for our new Women's Group member. As on every occasion when a new member joins Group I do not mention her by name until she has introduced herself. This is to protect her anonymity in case she should choose to use a different name (so far this never has been the case). I also gave apologies for absence. I noticed a general unease and looks exchanged between Group members when I gave Terri's apology for her second consecutive absence, but nobody offered any feedback on their thoughts or feelings about this, perhaps because this meeting was the first time of meeting the new Women's Group member, Dawn, and their loyalties were towards Terri, no matter the concern she was causing them, they now had an attachment to her.

Dawn said that she was happy to check in first and 'get it over with', as she said with a smile and her American accent obvious. She told us that she was there because she had had a battle with a gambling addiction that had been a part of her life since she was 15 years old. At first it had been a slot machine problem when she had discovered them in amusement arcades whilst on a cruise with her family. She had made the 'big mistake' of trying out gambling online three years ago and that was when things had really got out of control. The debts had piled up, she told us, and she had felt increasing pressure as she was too afraid to tell her husband and so attempted to continue to meet their financial obligations by taking

> *out more and more credit, then gambling from the pressure of trying to pay it off (there were lots of encouraging and sympathetic nods from around the room as she spoke). She told of how she had entered therapy wanting to stop gambling before she shared her problem with her husband. That through the 24 weeks of therapy she had achieved her aim and now had told her husband about her addiction. She was in Women's Group because she had identified in therapy that she needed to learn how to get close to people. That she was friendly and well thought of in her job, but that her professional self and cheery persona were like a suit of armour, a way of keeping others away from her vulnerabilities.*

Dawn had already taken a step forward in working towards what she wanted, because she had already allowed us to know how she defended herself from intimacy, and in so doing had rendered her defence less powerful as she could potentially hide less well now we all knew her disguise. The desire to hide her gambling from her husband until she could present it to him in the past tense is very familiar to me in my work with women and problem gambling. Many women feel so afraid of revealing their gambling addiction for fear of the reactions of those close to them. They fear, as we have seen so far, judgements, lack of understanding because it is gambling and not drink, not drugs, and ultimately abandonment. They fear the pain of their own guilt and shame as they face the shock and shattered trust in those that they love, but could not put first because gambling had them under its addictive spell. They wonder and hope that if they might present themselves as a woman who 'was' rather than 'is' a gambler that they might lessen the odds of the destruction of the relationship. They hope to fast forward through the mess in the middle stuffed with anger, uncertainty, fear and the pain of saying 'I have a gambling addiction' to saying 'I have recovered from a gambling addiction'. They hope that if they can offer evidence that they are to be trusted, because they have changed, they might just save the relationship. Gambling addiction is shrouded in secrets and lies and hidden from the view of those close, and so the desire is to present tangible evidence that it is no longer in existence.

> *Following Dawn's check in everyone else took their turn. During check in and for the remainder of our meeting it was as if we had rewound time on the little silver clock that marked our every moment to the first couple of weeks of meeting. The talk was very much about the type of gambling that each woman used and the financial and*

> *practical impacts. Any emotions that were touched on were directly related to gambling; anxieties at money lost, anger at the gambling industry for providing female friendly products and advertising. Despite this return to more superficial topics, Dawn seemed to be welcomed and accepted into Group. At check out, Janet spoke directly to Dawn and said that she did not know how she would feel about a new member starting, but that she was okay. I also invited everyone to say how they felt about Terri's absence. Paula made a comment, saying that she hoped that she was all right and that she would come back next week and Helen nodded her agreement saying 'the longer you stay away, the harder it is to come back. I know from when I missed a couple of meetings'.*

It is natural to the pattern of Women's Group that if a new member joins an established group that the depth of disclosure changes for a while to a more superficial level and discussions centre once again around topics that are bonding for Group such as gambling and its consequences and, yes, even the demonisation of the gambling industry. I have heard many plots and plans to put bombs under bookmakers and send petitions of complaint about the industry to the government, so strong are the feelings of women against the gambling industry when they first start treatment. These feelings usually decrease in correlation with the increase of each woman's self-understanding that her gambling problem was sparked by problems in her life, rather than the existence of the gambling industry (Karter, 2013). When bonding needs to be achieved in Women's Group, uniting against the gambling industry, which is put in the role as the foe that takes advantage of and exploits the vulnerable, can be a way of achieving such cohesion. Often as the process of Group moves on and women are open to greater challenge, we have identified that, although there might of course be genuine anger at the gambling industry, the gambling industry might too stand in for others in life who have abused and exploited so many of the women who attend meetings. Group members unite and transfer onto the gambling industry all of the anger and frustration they have suppressed for fear of the consequences were they to aim it truly where it belongs.

Anger is an emotion that, when felt and finally expressed within Women's Group, can be a powerful force. Anger is energy and the energy equal to it; to suppress it has often been a cause of depression for the women I meet. When it is finally expressed, ultimately it is a release and a relief and a step forward in recovery for the woman who has gambled to squeeze it back down. I therefore welcome its arrival in Women's Group and even its being directed at me. With the best will in the world and with all my best efforts, I will make mistakes; I will let down and disappoint those I am responsible for in Women's Group. I make it clear as soon as opportunity arises that I invite and welcome each woman telling me exactly how she feels about me and her response to my behaviour. This is not easy at first for the majority of women. I represent, albeit unconsciously, an authority figure, a mother figure. When we are children, we need to see our parents as capable and in control, as super human beings incapable of mistakes. We need to hang on tightly to that image of them because we need to believe that we can trust in their parenting abilities and relax into being taken care of by them. For the many women who arrive in Group as a childlike self, their need to see me as infallible is just as strong. In the early weeks I am careful not to reveal too much of myself, as they need to have as much confidence in me as therapist and in their Women's Group as possible, in order to completely let go of the false sense of something to cling to offered by gambling, and to step over and stand firm on the rock offered by Group whilst they build firm foundations for life outside. As the weeks go by and women grow more confident and competent in the realm of self-care, both inside and outside of Group, their needs in relation to me as therapist change, just as do the needs of the young adult in relation to their parents. At that stage it can be healthy that they view me as human and capable – yes, of being reliable, professional and trustworthy – but fallible and feeling, too. Many women speak of how this encourages them; that despite error and illness they see me as a functioning person and that if being a functioning woman meant being 'perfect' it would never give them hope of moving towards that way of being themselves.

Anger towards me therefore is an expected part of the developing phases of Women's Group and if expressed openly can move forward a woman's recovery in leaps and bounds as she uses the confidence and trust in herself that she gains from challenging peers in her Group, and myself, and resolving issues that previously would have festered and driven gambling urges. Anger within Group towards another member, and/or with me, which is unexpressed in the long term eats away at a woman's relationship with her Women's Group, and her relationship with me, and also with herself as she proves to herself once again that she cannot trust herself to stand up for herself when needed. The danger is that instead of expressing her anger within Women's' Group she will suppress it in the way that is only too familiar to her and run away from Group so that she does not have to face it, just as she has run to hide from it in gambling. Sadly that is what Terri chose to do. Before our next meeting Terri sent a letter to me saying that she had made a decision not to return to Women's Group. She said that she felt she had managed in the three weeks away from meetings and that she still felt that she did not fit in and that I favoured other members of the Group and had not stood up for her when she had been accused of not being her true self.

I was saddened that Terri had felt unable to return to Group and to talk through her thoughts and feelings. I reflected on my own behaviour around the things she mentioned and the fact that, while these things might have been truly her perspective, I was aware that she felt her father had stood back and allowed her mother to abuse her, so was she in some way expecting me to do the same? She had sadly grown up feeling that she was not wanted within her family group; might it not be natural that these feelings would arise in Women's Group? Indeed, perhaps in any social group Terri became a part of? If she had stayed and talked to me of her feelings and worked through these issues she might have gained greater personal insight and a chance to improve her relationship with me and her Group, and to develop her relational skills. These skills applied in life outside might have positively changed the dynamics of her pattern of interpersonal relating and therefore given her every chance of continued strong recovery from gambling addiction. Sadly, we will have to sit with uncertainty about how Terri moved on with her life after Women's Group.

Let us stop and think for a moment, before reading further, to contemplate: what do we each imagine happened to Terri after she left Group?

I would imagine each of us reading would have created a different story for what Terri's future held. What we imagine is likely based on our own hopes and fears formed by our life experience. How we feel about the sudden loss of a relationship will be informed again by our personal experience of loss. If we experience abandonment or rejection do we feel anger, anxiety or sadness? Do we blame the absent other for leaving us, or do we blame ourselves for the other leaving?

> When at the next meeting I passed on Terri's notice of leaving Women's Group it was met with silence at first. I asked for reflections on thoughts and feelings around Terri's decision and Janet was first to speak saying that she was not surprised. She said that addiction was hard to beat and, closing her eyes, she prayed that God would protect Terri from temptation from further addiction. She added that she knew she had said Women's Group was scary because it was like family, but that out there alone in the world was a much scarier place to be.
>
> I was aware that Paula looked unsettled when Janet spoke of the scariness of family. She was shifting uncomfortably in her chair and

said that she hoped it was not something that she had said that had influenced Terri's decision. She reflected on how there had been a week when she herself had questioned whether to continue with Group because she was going through a period of feeling vulnerable and wondered if hearing the stories of others in Group was making her feel worse. Perhaps here Paula's 'Don't tell' rule, which she had been given by her mother's silencing of her when she reported her childhood abuse, had been activated. She had told us of how she was feeling and now imagines she has evidence that something bad happens if we tell; she has been abandoned by a member of her Women's Group as she feared abandonment by her family.

Sarah quickly came in at this point and, leaning forward in her chair, looked at the same time upset and angry. She said to Paula 'Yes, but the difference is that you said that was how you were feeling and so we all said to you to stick with it (Women's Group). She (Terri) hasn't done that and instead she's left us all to think about her again, to worry what she's up to again'. I said to Sarah that I was aware that Terri's leaving was bringing up strong emotion for her and asked if she was feeling one thing she had identified? Worried? Sarah began to cry and said that yes, she was worried and felt bad that she had spoken badly of Terri in the last meeting and that now she had gone missing. At the same time, she felt angry too, because it was hard work to be in Group. 'Every week I come here and there are times I really don't want to be here, because I face my own crap. But I come because I want to sort it out. And now she (Terri) clears off and I have to worry about her too'. I said gently to Sarah that I imagined it must be very hard for her, when she had so much responsibility at home for so many others, to feel that she now should worry about someone else, too. She started to sob, saying yes, it just was not fair. It felt like she would never, ever get out from underneath the pile of people and responsibilities that were pinning her down and squeezing the life out of her.

Helen looked highly anxious and said that she too felt bad and wondered if she had said too much. She said she knew that sometimes she could 'seem a bit mad' and that sometimes she 'talked too much' and that she wished she had allowed more time for Terri.

To encourage an open flow of self-expression, I speak in Women's Group of how we can never know how anything we say might affect another. Therefore, rather than each member attempting to take responsibility for every other member by censoring what they say, it is better that each member takes responsibility for their own feelings by practising sharing with Group, speaking out if they have been hurt or angered by something that has been said.

We see how a strong theme in the individual responses to Terri's leaving was self-blame, and to imagine that it was something that they said that had caused Terri to leave them, that maybe they had taken too much space, said too much. Just as earlier in this chapter we, the reader, not knowing what happened to Terri after she left Women's Group, are invited to imagine, and from our past experiences project onto the blank screen of our uncertainty, familiar scenes from our past, so too do the members of the Women's Group we follow. The perceived rejection and/or abandonment by another Group member brings with it uncertainty. Uncertainty being one of the most fearful experiences for most Group members, the little girl inside each of them is scared. This little girl feels that she must have done something wrong to deserve being abandoned. Group members imagine that they have broken the 'Please others' or 'Don't tell' rule by saying too much; imagining they have taken up too much time and space is common. As we have seen, gambling addiction has been a way of keeping those rules, by suppressing voices at a volume at which they have been inaudible even to the women to whom they belong. We see in Sarah's reaction the inner conflict experienced by so many women who attend Women's Group, as they have struggled to live life by 'Please others'. In Sarah we see her confusion of worrying for Terri, while feeling resentment at 'having' to do so. These resentful feelings, which again in the past have been denied by gambling too much time, too much money, until she felt too guilty to feel the resentment that had driven the addiction.

As infrequently as it happens past the first six weeks of Women's Group process, when it does I am always sad to lose a member from Women's Group. That woman has lost her opportunity to gain self-understanding and understanding of what drives her addiction by standing and facing the fears induced by relationship that have sent her running scared. The loss is often frightening and painful for the remaining Group members, but what is gained for them is insight to how their past experiences of damaged and damaging attachments continue to influence their here-and-now relationships and therefore their drive to addiction as a safe haven.

As our new Group member, Dawn, illustrated when she spoke of Terri's leaving 'I didn't get to know the lady, so I guess it doesn't affect me. You guys had a relationship with her'. Once we take the risk of attachment, we take the risk of loss. That is the risk so many in Women's Group have avoided by having their closest relationship as that with gambling addiction. Living through the scary and painful time of loss of a fellow Group member helps each to gain experience that it is possible to tolerate those feelings of loss, rejection and abandonment. Experiencing alongside this that it is the sharing with others with whom one is now attached that makes the loss easier to bear provides a real-life, in the here-and-now example of how the benefits of real relationship might just make it a risk worth taking.

Chapter 5

Working towards closure

We began Chapter 1 with the statement that gambling addiction in women is all about relationships. I have found through clinical experience that the cure for gambling addiction is a little like finding the cure for an allergy, in that it requires exposure to many possible triggers for the allergic reaction to identify what has caused the problem and to know whether it is best treated by avoidance or by gradual exposure to what it is that causes the bad reaction. Women's Group has proved to be a safe environment in which the women can identify their own particular emotional and psychological triggers for their cravings to gamble to flare up. We have seen how difficult the journey is to the first Group meeting as for each woman it requires finding the courage to face others and to face herself in relation to others. To face the truth of the mess that gambling addiction has made of her life, her finances and her relationships. She will face the regrets for loss of time and opportunity. In essence, she asks herself to do the opposite to which all instinct has told her is necessary to her survival, which has been to run and hide from the reality of life, from the thoughts that tell her she is living an inauthentic life, betraying herself. To blur the edge of reality with the slot machine, or the computer screen, or the Smartphone, to render her for that time dumb and numbed to her inner misery and ever growing outer chaos.

We have seen that in Women's Group, as trust and confidence grows, she will face herself, as others in Women's Group hold a metaphorical mirror for her, and they reflect back to her what they see. As in the Women's Group we are following, she will face all the difficulties that come with being in intimate relationship, all the mess and pain associated with developing attachment and inevitable separation and loss (Bowlby, 1986) Let us not forget that what she will also experience is the joy that comes with such attachment, the things that keep us returning for another go at relationship of all kinds, be they romantic and sexual or friendships and family; the support, the fun, the sense of security and stability and belonging, the outlet for emotional expression that comes with our healthy relationships. The things that make life feel so much more rewarding and so much easier to bear when it is not so. In all, the things that make us so much less likely to pick up an addiction to hold on to because we feel that there is little else in life to feel attached to, or to bring us shelter from life's storms. She has challenged the rules of 'Don't be close', 'Don't tell', 'Please others' and 'Be perfect' and found that, despite the childhood beliefs that she had carried, that something bad will happen if she breaks those rules, that not everyone will abandon or reject or punish her when she does. That, in actual fact, often something very good happens, in that she develops healthier and closer relationships with others and with herself.

Women's Group is not all 'doom and gloom' as we might imagine with women who have such a compilation of traumatic stories. In fact, for each woman attending, as time progresses and more gambling-free time is gained, as the hurt Child inside of her heals, she has a greater capacity not only for clarity of thought and feeling but for a sense of humour, the ability to be playful and to enjoy the lighter side of life. In the same meeting, along with perhaps deep exploration of inner pain past and future and reflections on recovery, we might hear the odd discussion of what is going on in the latest soap episode, or humorous stories of someone's pet dog. This could of course be interpreted as avoidance, and indeed if we had half an hour exclusively on someone's pet escapades it might be so. In the appropriate context, however, there is a true healthiness to these interactions. They are about real life in the outside world, the world outside of the frozen nothingness of gambling addiction. They represent a woman feeling confident enough and free of fear enough to be playful again. These conversations say that she sees herself as beginning to belong not only to Women's Group but to a wider world group. She is saying that she is no longer completely blinded by preoccupation with her addiction and its terrible consequences; that she is starting to notice again the detail of the world around her. I have sometimes playfully commented in Women's Groups that there might be a market for a 'Women's Group Book of Helpful Hints' as women have advised each other on practical life issues from the best money-saving travel tips, to how to make a humane mouse trap! Indeed, once they are free of problem gambling I find that I tend to be in the company of some of the most resourceful women I have had the pleasure to meet; they are survivors, having survived both the misery and anxiety of the highs and lows of gambling addiction, which was a way of surviving the horrors that they were attempting to hide from. A sign of a healthy Women's Group at around the ten-month period is one in which gambling is very rarely mentioned, the focus is now all on maintaining recovery and that of course is done through maintaining a healthy lifestyle and lots of real living.

When we return to Women's Group at ten months into the process we might understand, then, all that each woman has invested in her relationships within Group, all that she has risked and gained and so therefore what she feels she stands to lose when faced with the end of Women's Group at the one-year closure point. Her fear was initially the attachment to others within Group and now the separation and the loss of her relationships with others in her Group.

One of the biggest hurdles for her to negotiate in order to allow herself to attend Women's Group was that of trust. She has now learned to trust in her Group and learned to trust in herself, but the trust she has both in herself and in others might still in some cases be limited to the boundaries of the Group. Can she trust herself to make good decisions without the support of Women's Group? Can she trust herself to remain gambling free without Women's Group? Can she trust herself to be discerning enough to know who to trust enough to let herself be close and to know who to keep out? The fear is now not of attachment to Group, because of it being such a high risk to trust, or because of the shame and guilt associated with being seen and heard when she fears that so much of her behaviour might be harshly judged, but of what happens when that now deeply valued attachment that has been such a source of support, and that she will associate with a strong recovery, is severed.

To make the separation process less of a severing and more of a gradual working towards acceptance of the need to let go, each week from the ten-month period of the process I will mention at the check in that we have a certain number of weeks left and encourage each member to talk about her thoughts and feelings regarding the ending. I will also focus on each member of Women's Group taking the skills that she has learned in Women's Group into life outside of Group. Earlier, I referred to the fact that Women's Group is a place to learn healthy relational skills, how to make friends, not a place to find friends, and as Group draws to an end the woman who has taken that on board and made efforts to build a strong social network outside of Women's Group, where appropriate to repair broken friendships and family relationships damaged by her withdrawal into the world of gambling addiction, will find the ending easier than the woman who has used Women's Group as her sole source of human contact. It may have been tempting to do so, as it is safe and relatively risk free. If she has used Women's Group as a way to take the edge off her need for closeness and not made efforts to rebuild life outside, the danger is that when Group ends, she will return to life much as it was before she entered Women's Group. She will not have used Group to its full potential, but merely just as she used gambling as a refuge from engaging fully with life, therefore almost as a cross addiction. When Group ends, she is at risk from cross addicting back to gambling. The women who go on to flourish when Women's Group closes are those who use it as a practice ground for life, to identify what it is that blocks them from going out into the world and engaging with life and relationships. They use Group to identify what it is that they truly want and need from life and have worked on developing skills such as assertiveness and conflict resolution and authenticity. They have grown to trust themselves by learning that they can discern who to let in and who to keep out. They have learned through Women's Group the difference in caring for others and sacrificing one's whole self for others. This has been helped by their learning to let go of guilt, through understanding what drove their gambling addiction and so experiencing genuine compassion and forgiveness for themselves. So often supported in this by the compassion and understanding of their fellow Women's Group members who have listened, and cared and accepted them, as opposed to judged and rejected them, as have many others, and indeed as they have been doing to themselves.

My role as therapist I have found to be key in modelling the art of caring for others, but also for one's self. We have seen and heard that for the typical woman who develops a gambling addiction there is a strong drive to 'Please others', which has driven her gambling addiction, as a way of getting in the metaphorical car and driving away when her overly demanding life and those equally demanding of her time and her inner resources leave her feeling so constricted that it is as though the very life is being squeezed out of her. Let us see this in action as we return to the Women's Group process at the ten-month period. We have just completed check in and I have raised the issue of our having eight more meetings left.

> *Sarah had told us that she had applied for a job, but that her husband was against her even attending the interview. He wanted Sarah to remain at home and to apply for state benefits so that she would be his paid carer. Sarah had now reached a point at which she had made a decision to leave her husband, but knew that in order to do so she needed an independent income. Her husband still controlled her finances and so she feared that if she went to the interview with his knowledge that he would stop her allowance, so she*

was considering going to the interview in secret. She felt guilty about doing so, because in order to lie to her husband she would also have to lie to her sons. Sarah said she was confused about what was the right thing to do. I asked Group as a whole if they had any thoughts on Sarah's dilemma. Dawn, who had been quick to establish a strong place and strong voice in Group said that she thought that Sarah had to put herself first for once. She went on to say that what she herself had realised from coming to Women's Group is that 'we' have all spent so much time trying to put everyone else's problems first and that was what the real problem was for everyone in Group. She said that she knew it was hard, because she herself fought a daily battle with feeling selfish every time she said 'no' to an unreasonable family request, but that she reminded herself, what was the choice?

'If the "no" doesn't come out of our mouths, it comes out of our bank accounts, because we end up gambling to ease the pressure' (Dawn)

Dawn went on to say that although her recovery from gambling addiction remained sound that it was at times very hard. She described having now clearly identified the triggers for her gambling urges as stress and the pressures of family life – both her extended and immediate family. That she wanted that to be a reason and not an excuse for her gambling. In other words, not to remain a passive victim to the stresses and strains and so justify gambling as an escapism, but to use the insight she had as to the reasons she gambled, to make changes that would help her to stop gambling. These changes included the way in which she responded to pressure and stress and so giving herself permission to make the choice not to obey the 'Please others' rule. When she was asked something by her family, she would now take a little time to listen to her inner voice and if her inner voice was saying 'no' then she would find the courage to speak the 'no' rather than a resentful 'yes'. 'Don't get me wrong', she added with a tense laugh, 'It's not all a walk in the park. Sometimes when I get home tired after work and the baby is crying, the cat hasn't been fed and my husband has done nothing to help, I still think "oh my dear God. Let me switch the computer on to gamble!" But I don't, because I know I will feel worse afterward. And that feeling happens less and less now'.

The other members of Group nodded and laughed with Dawn, they all recognised so well the inner conflicts of which she spoke. Sarah looked thoughtful and after a short silence said, 'You see, I want to be like you. I want to have a job. I want to be like you, Liz'. I asked Sarah what she saw in me, or imagined about me, that she *would like for herself? She said that it seemed to her that I loved my work, and that she knew that I spoke at conferences and was getting on with my career. She added that even more than that, she would love to be like me in how I looked after myself. That she could see that I cared about the Women's Group, but she also saw that I did not get completely hooked in to carrying everybody's problems. She gave the example of Terri and how she had left so suddenly. 'You cared about her, but you didn't get sucked completely in. I would have been up all night worrying and phoning her, running after her and making myself ill. But you kept to your boundaries and what you thought was right for you and us (Women's Group). I just worry that I'm not going to get there. I've got eight weeks left and I still haven't got there'.*

We might take two very important points from what Sarah was saying. One is the importance of what I as Group therapist model to Women's Group through my own behaviour, and the other the additional pressure that is created by the countdown to Women's Group closure. By this stage of Women's Group process, my role is likely to be one where I am trusted and my position as being part of Group, but at the same time on the periphery, accepted. For Sarah, she aspired to have the qualities of being able to choose when to care for others, without losing all sense of herself. As Group therapist, I am aware that my every interaction in Group is being watched and assessed. In Chapter 8 I will go into greater detail about the professional and personal qualities and ways of being that I have consistently found are valuable to cultivate for a Women's Group therapist. For now it is important to emphasise again the value of being seen to be a *feeling* being. As we have seen so far, most women are in Women's Group because they have certain feelings, which to them are intolerable, and that they have avoided by dissolving them for a time through gambling addiction. To witness that I feel and have empathy with the women who share their stories with me, that I care but that my care giving is not compulsive, and in doing so I keep a strong sense of myself and so am not lost in the needs of the other is encouraging, for women such as Sarah, to aspire to do the same. If the women in Group can witness me setting boundaries and not being pushed, pulled or manipulated into breaking them, exhausting myself, or running on empty it communicates that it might be okay for them to do the same. If they can witness me taking care of myself as well as them, and sometimes putting myself first, by taking a sick day when I am ill, or taking a holiday, and they do not reject or abandon me for doing so, it might help their confidence that just maybe if they did the same others they are close to might not reject or abandon them either. The sky does not have to fall in if we do not 'Please others'.

The second point raised by Sarah was the pressure she felt under to 'get there'. Some women fear that they will have in some way failed if they do not leave Women's Group having created the perfect life. If they have lived by the 'Be perfect' rule, this can be a particular issue. For any of us, the positive about having limited time is that it causes us to reflect on how we might best use that time. It is valuable to encourage women with such anxieties about Group ending to focus on exactly what they have already achieved and what they would like to achieve in the time that they have left in Group. It is helpful to remind them of what their personal agenda was when they first entered Women's Group and to explore whether if it is still high on their agenda to achieve that aim. It can be incredibly powerful to invite other Group members to help look at how far one member has come by reflecting to her the changes that they have witnessed. Often, I have heard touching and powerful examples given of the differences they see in her, since her beginning of Group; this can be incredibly good for her self-esteem and also for her belief in her own power to continue to make positive change. Very often she might be so used to self-criticism and so driven by an overdose of guilt and 'Be perfect' that she will see only what she has *not* achieved, and be blind to all that she has. If her goal might not be realistically achievable within the time left in Women's Group, perhaps she might look at how to continue towards her aim in life after Women's Group closure. To emphasise that her growth and development and continued recovery is a *process* and that Group is not an exam to pass or fail is key, as is to encourage her to measure the value of the changes she is making not just in terms of gambling-free time, but in the awareness of her inner world of thoughts and feelings and how she is engaging in the outer world; as we will now be so aware at this stage of following Women's Group, the real and lasting change with gambling addiction is forged beneath the surface layer of the addictive behaviour. Iron-like resistance to the addiction is created first through changes to her relationships, relationship with herself, then others in her Women's Group and then with relationships in her wider world. This is the 'women's work', which positively affects long-term change to patterns of gambling addiction behaviour. She ends her destructive, complex relationship with gambling addiction.

Fear can freeze, and the approaching end of Group can cause a halt in their process for some women as they become so focused on fearing what might happen when Group ends that they cease to make productive changes to ensure that life is okay beyond Women's Group closure. It is therefore vital to continue to encourage open discussion about fears around Group ending to keep this conscious where members are able to work with managing these fears.

Flight is a response to fear favoured by most women who attend Women's Group, which has of course been actioned by their taking flight into gambling addiction, and a danger is that the fear response triggered by Women's Group closure may mean that some women drop their attendance in Group. It is rare that a woman who has been a committed member throughout the entire process will leave early because of the thoughts and feelings brought about by closure, but to begin to sporadically attend meetings, when before she has been a regular attendee, is much more likely.

We are now back in Women's Group with four meetings left, including today. Helen has apologised in check in for missing the last meeting owing to having to let a plumber in. She had missed the meeting of two weeks before because of feeling unwell. This was unusual for Helen, she rarely missed meetings. When I had asked her to reflect on any thoughts and feelings she might have about the impending closure of Group she appeared very agitated and found it hard to sit still in her chair. Janet was watching her intently. Janet sometimes would say very little in meetings, but when she did speak would often be very insightful and was often accurate in her reflections to others of their behaviour and what she imagined was going on for them in their inner world. She said that she was thinking that maybe Helen was gambling again and that was why she had stayed away, or maybe she did not like thinking about the end of Women's Group and maybe that was why she had not come to meetings in the last few weeks, to avoid the ending?

'Sometimes it's easier if we don't get close to anyone, then they can't hurt us. I know I do that myself sometimes. But I am so tired of doing that now. I have been lonely all my life, even with so many children. I don't want to be lonely anymore. Not anymore'. (Janet).

Helen said that she had gambled a small amount, about ten or twenty pounds online on two occasions since the last meeting, but that she was feeling okay about that. She had managed to stop herself 'beating herself up' about gambling. Listening to others in Group, she had realised that only made her feel miserable and so more likely to continue gambling to shut out the critical things she would say to herself. She now knew from experience that drawing a line underneath a relapse and making a determined effort not to dwell on it was a way to move on to more gambling-free time. She was silent and thoughtful for a while and then said 'I've just got to make sure that I can do this by myself. I can't rely on you lot all the time, so I thought I'd see . . . test myself . . . am I going to be all right when I can't come here anymore?'.

The uncertainty raised by the ending of Women's Group has engendered fear in Helen and her response has been to take flight. Uncertain as to her abilities to manage recovery without Women's Group she has tested herself. This is not unusual and many women fear relapse to gambling so greatly, wondering if it will be triggered by their inability to manage the trials of life without Group support, that they do as Helen did and miss meetings to test their resilience. I have known of one or two women who have gone so far as to risk recovery and gamble to see if the addictive feelings are still lying in wait to overwhelm them. They have felt that by putting themselves in that situation they are more in control than if they passively waited for the predatory cravings that they imagine to be stalking them in the darkness of uncertainty to pounce and if this happens, still to have Group back up.

Occasionally, the fear of separation and loss, and the feeling of being left alone without care and attention, are stronger even than the fear of relapse to gambling, and relapse is brought about intentionally, either consciously or subconsciously, as a desperate attempt to ensure ongoing care and attention. If this occurs, it is less about self-sabotage and more about survival. The woman who is willing to risk her precious and hard won recovery is likely to have struggled to find a strong enough Adult self during the Women's Group process in order to have faith that she can manage life in the world outside. In my experience this difficulty has arisen because she has suffered particularly damaging childhood experiences and has been deprived of even basic love and attention in childhood. She has possibly learned, through lonely and painful experience, that the only way to gain any level of attention is through negative behaviour or hurting herself. One woman described how the only time she remembered, as a child, even the tiniest drop of warmth, care and attention from her mother was when she was very ill with pneumonia. If as a result of such poor parenting she has spent many years within the mental healthcare system, for example, she is likely to struggle with believing that she has the capacity to cope without structured care and be living life by 'Don't be well', 'Don't grow up' as a way of trying to ensure the care that she had the right to expect in childhood, but so sadly never experienced. The little girl inside of her fears that if she gets 'well', if she 'grows up', that she will never, ever get the love and care she so longs for.

For Helen, like so many of the women we have met here in our Women's Group and in the many others I have worked with over the years, we might understand how control would feel so important. They have experienced uncertainty as heralding not special surprises but sinister shocks and so will try to read the road ahead to head off predicted dangers. When Women's Group closure nears, it is natural for each woman that anxieties are triggered by uncertainty of what lies ahead, which in turn can trigger old defence mechanisms, such as taking flight, to test whether by withdrawing again from relationship that she will regain control of how she *feels* about the ending and the separation and loss. This is healthy and a golden key of the process. If she can find courage and be encouraged to stay and to face these fears the process of the ending can help her to learn so much more about herself and the pain of separation and loss that she has been avoiding by building herself a wall built brick by brick of preoccupation with gambling, the anxieties and depression of its aftermath, the self-exile resulting from guilt and shame. All have prevented her from being truly close to another because, as Janet says, if we do not get close, we do not get hurt. Cut off from our social groups, what we *do* get is isolated, lonely and vulnerable to predators like addiction. We need to be able to face our fear of separation and loss and to tolerate those feelings if we are to allow ourselves to stay safe within close, healthy relationship.

The fight response to the fear of Women's Group ending might be dramatic. As we have discussed, most women who attend find it hard to openly express anger, having been used to suppressing it by gambling, having experienced anger used in inappropriate or often even abusive ways. Once they are able to access their anger they often free up behind the log jam a raging torrent that has been surging inside them over many years. It can take time for this to settle to a natural, healthy flow of expression of angry feelings as they arise. A striking example of this was when I was running a Women's Group for problem gambling for a treatment agency a few years ago. The agency needed to close the Women's Group and, appropriately as Group therapist, I delivered this news to Women's Group. One woman who had at first strongly resisted even the very idea of attending Women's Group but had courageously attended and gone on to become a member committed to both the Women's Group process and her own became so angry at the closure of Group that she made complaints to senior management and trustees of the agency in question and started a petition to keep her Group open, which she took as far as parliamentary ministers. The positives for the woman who did this were in that her tendency before her hard work over seven months in Women's Group would have been to suppress her anger by gambling. In Group, as her thoughts, feelings and actions unfolded over four weeks, we identified that as well as being a healthy expression of her anger; in her strong reaction there was too an equally strong element of avoidance of her more vulnerable thoughts and feelings about the ending. When we are angry, we can feel much stronger than we do if we feel sad. If we have disturbing associations with feeling vulnerable, fighting battles can be a way of hiding our fearful, sad and vulnerable self behind angry attack. It is valuable for all of us to work out the underlying motivation choosing our battles, and a part of the role of Women's Group and myself as therapist, is to facilitate this if the urge to fight is triggered by ending.

> We return to the Women's Group meeting we left with Helen feeling she needed to prove to herself that she could cope alone. Paula told Helen that she knew how hard it was to build a full life and that it had taken her many years to get to the place where she was now, where she had enjoyable activities and a social life outside of the world related to addiction and mental-health service-related activities. She said that it made sense to her, however, that Group needed to end and that all services had to limit their provision. She then went on to list in detail and discuss with Helen whom she might contact to find activities to enrol in, and the kind of things that she might do. All of this was helpful to Helen, but I was focusing less on the detail of what Paula said, and more on the way in which she was saying it. She was speaking with a very concise, professional tone and with authority. I wondered if Paula was coping with any difficult thoughts and feelings she might have about our ending by returning to her professional self, which she had found gave her strength to cope with uncomfortable emotion before. I decided at that time not to challenge her directly on whether that was what she was doing, but instead commented on how the conversation seemed to have gone to a very practical, rational level and wondered if that might feel a safe place to be at that time, as it was pulling us out of uncomfortable feelings that might be present around Group ending.

As therapist, there is a need to make moment-by-moment decisions about the value of interpreting someone's behaviour, or challenging her. When managing endings, sometimes it is natural and even healthy that certain defences are called on as a way of managing the process of separation and loss. Again it is all in the art of balance. A complete denial of thoughts and feelings around ending of course is unhealthy and were I to go along with no reflection to her of what I see, I would be merely colluding in her avoidance of reality and perhaps confirming by my doing so that yes, these feelings are much too scary to talk about and best left alone. Paula, however, was well aware from previous conversations that she used her professional self at times to rationalise and so to manage intense emotional difficulty. Women's Group is of course built on foundations of truth faced in relationship with oneself and others, but if someone has faced the truth of her defences, and when and how she uses them, there may be no harm if they help her get through tough times here and there, when she occasionally and consciously calls on them. Working with Women's Groups for Problem Gambling I think very carefully before commenting or interpreting any body language. I am always aware that I am likely to be working with a group of women who have good reason to be cautious about any degree of physical intimacy, as often issues of sexual or physical abuse are present. Commenting too often on body language can cause women to freeze physically for fear of what I may be reading in their movements. They may feel objectified, that they are there purely for my observation. I have found it more valuable to keep for my own awareness of her process what I see in body language unless I feel certain that the woman concerned is resilient enough to take something positive from what I say I see physically in her. While speaking of body language and it being interpreted I am aware of the fact that women who are the survivors of abuse are hyper-vigilant to perceived danger and I am mindful of my own movements and of maintaining respect for personal space.

> *Dawn said that she guessed it must be really difficult for everyone who had been in Women's Group from the beginning to have to say goodbye. She was sad that it was ending, but she felt positive too, that it was a new beginning and a chance to get out there in the world and make a new start, to put gambling behind her. Janet asked me whether I ever ran groups for longer than one year and was it entirely up to me whether Group ended? If so many of them were feeling sad about ending, could I maybe extend the Group time by another couple of months? I replied to Janet that yes, the decision was mine and that yes, I had on occasion run Women's Groups for longer than one year, but that the time any Women's Group ran was agreed at the very start and that I did not think it was in anyone's best interests to extend the time we had left. I asked how Janet felt about that: 'Disappointed. I feel disappointed, but I understand you have your rules and your reasons'. I said that maybe there was room*

for both. To understand that there were reasons for my decision, but also to feel something that maybe conflicted with her thoughts, such as disappointment. I said that I could understand if anyone might feel disappointed, upset or even angry with me as I had the authority to change the situation, but was sticking to the boundaries of what we had agreed.

Helen said that she liked it that I would not extend the closure date. It helped her to feel secure and to trust me, because she knew where she stood with me. She liked that I was consistent, even if she sometimes felt cross because I would not give her what she wanted. Helen said she remembered the meeting in the first couple of months when she had asked if we could have themed group meetings and we had all discussed the possibility, but that I had said I would not run themed meetings as I felt it would not be good for anyone, because it would be a way of controlling what was going to happen in meetings. I said it would replicate gambling addiction, in as much as it would interfere with the process of dealing with uncertainty and learning to sit with and process whatever thoughts and feelings might arise at any time. She said that she had felt a bit annoyed with me at the time.

As we draw to closure, I give as many appropriate opportunities as possible for Women's Group to share their feelings about me in relation to it. As the ending approaches, it may be hard for any woman to do so, but for different reasons from at the start of the process when it was hard for her to be emotionally expressive because feelings were in some cases buried by gambling addiction so deep for so long as to be unidentifiable. Or because of fear of the consequences of challenging authority – a parental figure, as I will often be seen in the role of. As we have seen in this book, by the middle months of Women's Group if all is working well, a woman will be much more able to express a wide range of feelings and strong emotion. By the latter stages of Group work however, she often feels a strong sense of loyalty to her Group and no less so to me. She may feel ungrateful if, for example, she acknowledges disappointment, anger, a sense of betrayal at finding that I have in the past run other groups for longer times. She may fear being disliked for displeasing me by expressing these feelings towards me; it is normal that Women's Group will evoke feelings of family, and so an element of 'sibling rivalry', and she may not want to take the risk of feeling like my least favourite 'daughter' when the end is approaching and there may be little time to repair any relational damage that she imagines. If she has had a particularly difficult relationship with her mother, the ending may raise feelings of abandonment and rejection directed towards me but, again, as when she was a child, she may fear expressing that, for what she imagines to be possible consequences. In her Adult self, with the evidence she has from her time in Women's Group, she may be certain that I will welcome her expression, her thoughts and feelings in relation to me, but the feared closure may tug at her remembered experiences of childhood and so her inner Child may be the strongest part of her in action. If so, she will attempt to protect herself in ways that she did in childhood, and pick up the Rule Book once again to follow 'Don't be close' or 'Don't feel'. Again, we reach the importance of encouraging her to test out what she *imagines* against what is the *truth*. To help her to reinforce that what she imagines might be based on past realities, and that the truth of the here and now might be quite different. The only way we test the validity of our thoughts is to put them into action. Women's Group is a wonderful, safe space in which to do just so, and in doing so free herself from the trap of gambling to silence those imaginings, which tell her the world is too dangerous a place to be so, as miserable as it is, better stay stuck tightly inside the gambling addiction trap.

If those of us reading take a moment to think about it, are we not probably all, at the very least, a little ambivalent about endings? We might prefer to think of endings as heralding bright new beginnings and opportunities, but they require change. Some of us will be more open to change than others and how we negotiate change often is based on our experience of change and our relationship endings. Having taken time to get to know our Women's Group members, we might have empathy with why they, and indeed all Women's Group members I have worked with, are particularly fearful of endings. We have heard of Janet's history of abandonment and Sarah's premature separation from her family. We know of Helen's unstable childhood with frequent house moves, her unpredictable father with whom she would suffer much pain of separation. Paula has spoken of the sudden loss of her much loved partner and devastating consequences of this. All are fearful of the pain of separation and loss and fear too that, if they do not negotiate it well, they will relapse to the nightmare world of gambling addiction, so doubling their pain. The knowledge of the approaching ending gives each woman a chance to get the best ending that she possibly can for herself, to work towards acceptance of the ending, to identify how she might be tempted to avoid her fears around it with fight, flight or freeze responses. The focus in meetings from ten months on is very much consolidation of the work that she has done, the personal insights she has gained as to the situations, thoughts and emotions that trigger gambling cravings. Extra attention is given to the way of relating with others in Women's Group and to ways in which she can get into action with her new awareness and skill set in her life outside. The little girl inside of her that fears separation and loss is given time and space to express the fearful feelings, but she is encouraged and supported to respond to what she is feeling from her Adult self. To take a proactive part in creating and responding to the Group closure and to make good, considered decisions throughout the process. Again, this is all part of healthy recovery as it moves so far away from the knee-jerk reactions to fear that have motivated her gambling problem and instils her with confidence in her own ability to negotiate life difficulties when they arise in life outside of Women's Group.

So, we arrive at the final meeting of the Women's Group who have allowed us to be a part of their recovery process. I was happy to find that all members were in attendance at the last meeting.

In fact, I have not yet experienced a final meeting where a woman who has been a part of the entire process has missed the meeting. By this stage her attachment is so strong that she feels an equally powerful sense of responsibility to Women's Group and would not wish to let anyone down by her absence. Again in terms of her self-confidence, which is essential for long-term recovery, she is proving to herself that after the chaos and roller coaster of crisis that was gambling addiction she can be reliable and that her presence and engagement psychologically, emotionally and practically are important to others. She is valued by a community and values this connection herself, which will give her a frame of reference in terms of what she is aiming to recreate in her relationships with the wider community outside of Group. In such a way, we see the wonderful benefits of Women's Group not just to the women who comprise the Group here today and others like it, but to society as a whole, which benefits from the Women's Group Ladies' (as this Group began affectionately to call themselves) enjoyment of and valuing of community and society, after the isolation that was so often both cause and consequence of gambling addiction. Vitally, each member will also be at that last meeting despite knowing that she might well feel sad at saying goodbye because she now knows, as a result of the process of Group, that to stand and face our feelings, even when they are uncomfortable, is the way to grow in emotional strength and therefore in immunity to gambling addiction.

Two weeks before closure, as always with the end of any Women's Group, I invited thoughts about how the members might like to mark the closure, pointing out that it is of course both an ending, which needs to allow for thoughts and feelings around it to be honoured, but at the same time a celebration of the work that has been done in Group over the year.

> *Paula has baked cakes and brought them to the meeting and had coordinated with Sarah in our last meeting so that Sarah brought savoury snacks and Janet some soft drink. There had been a humorous request from Dawn that they might be allowed to bring wine, but I had light-heartedly explained that I did not think that appropriate after a year of working so hard at being with our feelings that we should now take the edge off them with a glass or two. Helen had then suggested that perhaps after the meeting they might all go for coffee or to the pub and asked me to join them. I had said that one part of me wished that I could do so, as I would love to join in with them, but that I cared enough about them and their wellbeing to disappoint myself and to say no. After all, what if they saw me differently, or found out something about me socially that there was then no time to process, because we had no more meetings?*
>
> *To the final meeting Helen had brought the words to a song she had written about the importance of friendship. She had rediscovered the ability and the pleasure of music and singing since reducing her gambling significantly to the occasional slip. The words of her song moved everyone in Group as she read it to us: 'When I came here I was dead, a walking emptiness, but you, strangers who became my friends, you saved me. You gave me hope, were always there, understood my fears, stayed through my tears, you saved me' (Helen).*
>
> *The hope, fears and tears that Helen spoke of were some of the ingredients that formed our last meeting. In equal measure were laughter and a sense of determination for each woman to take the skills she had developed in Group and to use them to continue to build healthy relationships with herself and with others. To remind herself what it was that she found valuable in Women's Group and to seek it out in life outside.*

So let us see where each of our Women's Group members is in her recovery process as we close with a final Check Out.

Paula

Paula had gambled on only three occasions of a few hours each, since the start of Women's Group. She was now finding that focus on art and craft activity and on academic study for an Open University course replaced the absorption that she found soothing in gambling online. This not only helped her to manage her gambling, but meant too that she had now had her longest period without hospitalisation or self-harming. She had improved relationships with her sisters and felt that this was helped by her feeling that she could now engage with her family while staying in her Adult self, rather than being reduced to fearful Child and 'Please others', and so was now gaining respect from her family who saw her as more than her mental health issues, a 'problem gambler', and valued her as a whole person. She was also regularly engaged in local community activities such as an art group and volunteering in her local charity shop. With a good support network in place, she felt confident about moving on from Women's Group.

Helen

Helen's gambling was greatly reduced to an occasional relapse when she felt highly stressed or anxious in her relationship with her partner, or when she had intrusive thoughts about her rape. Having experienced being accepted in Women's Group when she disclosed the consequences of her gambling, and the life issues that drove it, including fears around how her sexuality might be received, Helen continued to work on healthily expressing her feelings with her partner. She had realised that the guilt she felt about her gambling-related debt and its impact on her partner had been driving her to be compliant, to over-compensate and then eventually to gamble again as a result of suppressing her authentic self and anger towards her partner's frequently controlling behaviour. Helen remained a little anxious about Women's Group closure, but her positive experience in Women's Group had given her a new frame of reference regarding counselling and therapy and had inspired confidence in her to go on to seek treatment in a group for women who had experienced rape or sexual abuse. She was convinced, as was I, as were her fellow Group members, that coming to terms with this issue would help her long-term recovery.

Janet

Janet remained gambling free as she had on entering Women's Group. Approaching her court case to decide whether she would be granted custody of her children who were still with foster parents, she faced an emotionally challenging time ahead. She continued to take comfort from regular church attendance and Anonymous meetings and so did not feel anxious about her recovery after Women's Group closure. She was able to say that she would miss everyone in that scary group that was like family, as she had described it early on in the process. She had experienced the value of breaking the 'Don't be close' rule, which, as we have seen and heard, always leaves any of us more vulnerable to addiction.

Sarah

Sarah was now well over two months gambling free and fiercely protective of her recovery. Now that she was gambling free and so her thoughts and feelings so much clearer, she had rediscovered her 'professional self' and how she could use those skills in day-to-day life to plan an exit route from her unhappy marriage. It was important to her to take a proactive role in this choice and to make a considered decision from her Adult self, rather than feel she was repeating that taking flight from her parents as she had done at the age of 15. Or taking emotional and psychological flight into gambling, because she could not give herself permission to physically leave, as she now recognised she had done. Women's Group helped to ease her guilt, which, as for Helen and for so many women, had then driven further gambling, by reflecting that they saw and understood reasons for their gambling as feeling trapped and controlled and a smaller suppressed self.

By this point of reading, along with the Women's Group members, I hope we have a greater understanding that what drives gambling addiction and what makes the difference to long-term recovery from gambling addiction is the quality of relationship, whether there are not enough relationships in life, or whether those that are there are damaging and destructive. The women who have shared their stories with us have experienced through Women's Group that what makes the positive difference to life, and so to feelings about life, and so the need to gamble to the point of implosion to escape life, are healthy, supportive relationships. And of course, a key is that our relationship with ourselves allows us to take the risk of being close.

Chapter 6

Life after Women's Group

For one year of each woman's life, Women's Group has been pivotal. Women's Group had been initially approached with trepidation as the journey to Group represented her journey through life thus far, in that the path had been a treacherous one, with hidden dangers lurking, often in the form of dangerous relationships. Just like Little Red Riding Hood, either in her childhood or perhaps in her vulnerability or naivety, as an adult woman, she had discovered a wolf in disguise once too often. Once she had firmly taken her place in Women's Group, it became the root out of which grew stronger understandings of herself in relation to others, of the barriers that she had constructed to block relationship and the reason for this, and of how gradually to deconstruct these barriers to begin to construct healthier attachments. These attachments, both to individual relationships and a community, have been invaluable in her continuing the process of detaching from her strongest and yet most darkly seductive and destructive relationship; that of addiction to gambling. In one year she has forged tools that she needs in the shape of relational and life skills, which will help her not only to let go of gambling but will also give her every reason to believe that her long-term recovery will continue, as they allow her to create a life away from the place she inhabited at the beginning of Group: the place of isolation and loneliness. These tools are not only practical skills, such as problem solving and assertiveness, but the ability to stand and face the fears that drove her addictive behaviour, to tolerate emotional intensity, to be able to soothe herself at times when her feelings threaten to overwhelm her and to trust in her ability to be discerning as to whom she might trust to ask for support when to stand alone feels lonely.

So in her year of Women's Group membership she has taken back much ground from gambling addiction. If we think of gambling as like a fast-spreading weed, which has been able to take over a garden that has not been attended or planted with anything beautiful that gave the weed less space to grow, in Women's Group that weed has now ideally been pulled out, roots and all, or at the very least largely cleared, to give her space to continue the work on planting what she truly wants in the garden of her life. Those of us who have ever managed even so much as a window box all know, however, that if we turn our backs for a while an unexpected wind can blow in seeds to sprout more of the weeds that we have worked so hard to remove. And the same with life itself; do we ever know what problems the winds of life might blow at us from a direction we did not expect? What makes the difference is how we are prepared for whatever might get blown our way and how we then manage it. So, what is it that a woman needs to do after Women's Group to ensure that her metaphorical garden, on which she has worked so hard, stays clear of the strangling, rapidly growing weed of gambling addiction? Experience has shown me that she needs to now focus less on the clearing of the weeds of gambling and more on prolific planting of an enjoyable lifestyle, which gives her contentment and support. The women who at one year follow up report gambling-free time, or the odd slip from which they have rapidly pulled back, are those women who have gone on to continue with the work that Women's Group started, and that of course is planting the seeds of good, strong healthy relationship and community activity. This quite simply helps them to have a full, enjoyable, stimulating, supported life that, when in full bloom, just leaves less room for the weeds of addiction to take over. If the weeds start to sprout up, these women have not only tools of their own but they have others to help them do the work of pulling them out.

The themes of each Group might be strikingly familiar and the level of support and understanding for each other always inspiring, but Women's Group of course is made up of individuals, and so in each Group the dynamics will feel slightly different from others that have gone before, as something new is always created each time we meet new people. In order to both ascertain the effectiveness of Women's Group and to offer an opportunity to check in, I offer optional one session, six-month and one-year follow up Women's Group meetings and/or one-to-one appointments. These follow up appointments are an opportunity to reflect on how well things are going, which has proven to be confidence inspiring and provides an injection of faith and hope of further change. It is also a chance to get back on track in any areas that are not going so well.

One-to-one appointments as an alternative, I offer for two reasons: the first very practical, that it is not always possible to find a mutually convenient time for up to seven ex-Group members plus myself to meet six months or one year along the line. Especially so if Women's Group has worked in the way in which it so very often does, and so the majority of women are busy getting on with full and productive lives. I am always delighted if a woman for whom life was an empty and meaningless void when she arrived in Women's Group, on trying to arrange the follow up meeting is genuinely struggling to find the time to attend a one-off meeting between a holiday, a regular social life, an enjoyable job and close family. How wonderful – her life is now so rich and varied. A one-to-one follow up option means that she need not miss out on the check in time should she be unable to attend the Group follow up. Very occasionally a woman may prefer not to attend a Women's Group follow up meeting. One reason might be if she has relapsed to gambling and feels shame and a sense of having let down her Group and fears that they will be disappointed in her. If she were to share this with me prior to the follow up meeting I would strongly suggest that she attends the Women's Group meeting again to challenge the old fears and beliefs that are likely to arise during relapse; that she will be judged and rejected. I am confident enough through my experience of my practice to believe that what she will receive from her peers is acceptance, understanding and encouragement to get right back on the recovery track. Another reason she may choose not to attend a Group follow up appointment is if she feels it will be emotionally challenging for her to meet with other women she has been so close with only to say goodbye again. This is indeed so rare as to have happened only three times. Most women are very keen to attend and to share their stories of where they are now along the recovery path and of course to hear the stories of others they developed such strong attachments to. Again, if they have used their year in Group to develop their outer world as well as their inner world they will have formed healthy attachments in life and no longer feel dependent on Women's Group. I have experienced follow ups as generally very positive meetings with much warmth demonstrated towards each other. I invite women to check in and check out as with regular meetings and themes tend to be reflections on what was gained from working together, what was and is missed about the process and an overview of how life is now.

A draft of the anonymous questionnaire that each woman is invited to answer is included in the next chapter of this book. Since 2006 I have facilitated 12 Women's Groups for Problem Gambling, each of the duration of one year or eighteen months and with a maximum of seven members in each Group. A total of 58 women completed the group process and out of those women who completed, 49 reported being gambling free at one year follow up. As *Working with Women's Groups for Problem*

Gambling was written more or less along with the Group process, I am unable to report on the progress at six months or one year of the members we have got to know. Sarah has kindly agreed to talk about how she felt about the Women's Group process we shared with her. This is a verbatim transcript from a recording that Sarah sent to me, having volunteered to talk about her Women's Group experience:

When I first came into Women's Group I thought I was prepared for what it was going to be like. I hadn't had counselling, I didn't want to sit and talk all about me, I wanted to be with other women who knew what it was like and I guess feel I was learning from them. Liz had talked to me about what to expect and I knew that we would talk about more than gambling. I think I imagined it would be like one of those films about group counselling when all you have to do is talk about something you kept a secret, just be honest and say 'I'm Sarah and I'm a gambler' and then you cry a bit, everything is okay and you go and live happily ever after.

I don't think I was ready for the level of honesty I heard from day one. So many of the women in my Group had such awful lives. I mean really awful lives, and at first I was thinking 'What have I got to moan about?' I've got a husband and kids, at least I'm not going to starve or be on the streets if I can't stop gambling. It was good for me though, because it made me think to myself, come on now, if they can stop gambling, people like Janet for example, who are going through so much, she might lose her kids, you can get there, too. I like that about Group, that everyone was at different stages in recovery, it gave me something to aspire to and showed me there is hope that I can get there, and then as I got further along, and others needed some encouragement at times, if I could do that it would show me that I had got somewhere, that actually I'd come a long way, but it's easy to forget that because you are so sick of yourself, you feel so guilty, it's like it's really hard to say 'well done' to yourself about anything. You feel you don't deserve it. Well I should say I felt I didn't deserve it. (Laughs.) Liz was always telling us to say 'I feel' and not 'you feel', if we are talking about ourselves, so we really make it feel real and about us, or me, there I go again! (Laughs.)

I think a big part of what worked in Group for me, it made it all real. I was there in a group of women who had a gambling addiction, no matter what was going on in our lives or what we had or don't have we were having our lives torn up by gambling. I remember for the first few weeks I'd just cry and cry because I'd sit and listen to the other girls and think about my life and things the other girls would say would make me think, hey, that's just what I feel. When Clare talked about feeling okay at work, then going home and feeling she was going nuts and wanting to gamble the minute she closed the front door. That's the thing we had more in common not just being gamblers, we all had difficult lives, we all tried to put on a brave face, and hide it by gambling. Things that Clare said helped me to see it was okay to face facts that I'm not happy in my marriage and haven't been for years. And nobody said 'You lucky cow, what have you got to complain about?', they all listened and understood and helped me to see it's horrible to have to live with somebody you don't love and feel close to and its okay to feel what I feel about it. I could see I was just as lonely as Janet and Paula, even though I had family. It's sad, and I do still feel a bit guilty, but at least now I'm facing that I can make a change. Gambling to forget about it just keeps me stuck in it, I ended up with no money to make the break, I had no energy to go, because I ended up so depressed and hating myself. I liked that we looked at the reasons for gambling, at first I said I didn't want to make excuses, but Liz always said that there were reasons for us all gambling and that's not the same as excuses. At first I wasn't sure if I believed her, but it's true. My reasons aren't pretty, but then whose are? I was just a mess, a big messy pile of anger and frustration and feeling guilty for feeling miserable when on paper I should have been happy. But I'm on my way, I've got a job! I feel so proud of myself and thanks to Liz and the girls for giving me courage to believe in myself. I've told my husband I want a divorce, I'm not sure he believes me, but I believe me. We are still in the same house until I save a bit to move out, but separate rooms, so that's a start and it's amicable. It seems easier for us both now we have faced up to what's really going on. And that's thanks to Group and to Liz because we always worked on talking about what was really going on with each other, instead of brushing it under the carpet. I remember we talked about if we keep brushing things under the carpet we end up with a great big hump, so it's just a big block between us and other people. Scary at times, I remember when it looked like there'd be a row, but we'd sort it out and we got through and we got closer after it. And, another great thing is . . . I haven't gambled for nearly two months. I feel so much better and stronger; I can hold my head high. I bought some new clothes for work; I've even had my hair done. I like me again. Anyway, so that's me. It was hard work and believe it or not, sometimes good fun [Group] and we had some

laughs as well as tears. I miss the girls and Liz, but I'm getting on with my life and that's what it [Women's Group] was all about.
(Sarah, one month after Women's Group closure)

It is wonderful to hear that Sarah is doing so well and I think that her last sentence referring to the fact that she is 'getting on with life and that's what it was all about' captures the essence, what it is that I have been emphasising makes the difference and of what makes Women's Group work well for the women who attend; it is a place to learn how to get on with life. Even though, just as Sarah says, not every woman may be sure of exactly *why* she is gambling, but almost every woman I've met is sure that she feels dependent on it to some degree for survival. Why then would she choose a method of treatment that takes away her gambling addiction, but does not offer her realistic hope, faith and confidence that she can at the very least cope with life without it? She wants not only to stop gambling, but to stop feeling the things that drive gambling addiction, such as feeling depressed, anxious, angry and frustrated and lonely. In Women's Group, Sarah has learned to cope with life and to move beyond gambling to survive to the desire and skills to thrive.

Sarah has put in place things that will create a framework of healthy routine, such as a new job. A routine makes a safe container to hold our lives together. If we have a strong routine, we not only have more structure and order, which is vital and reassuring after the chaotic world of gambling addiction, but it is confidence inspiring. It provides a sense of attachment to something strong and sound, so will help with the transition from the unhealthy attachment to gambling addiction. During work towards closure, a routine will help a woman with the process of separation from Women's Group and then will give her the feeling of being attached to something strong and sound that will help her to take what will at times feel like a risk of creating a fulfilling, productive and authentic life. Sarah became aware during her experience of Women's Group that it was the loss of power that she felt at living an inauthentic life to appease both her family and her guilt that led to gambling as both suppression of *and* expression of her angry and frustrated feelings. A silent and invisible expression of her rage at being seen heard and valued only with the condition that she 'Please others'. Many women post-addiction associate gambling with risk and then are understandably cautious and risk averse once gambling addiction has been removed and life becomes more ordered. Women's Group works towards the understanding that gambling was not risk, but a way of avoiding taking the risk of engaging in life, which then in desperation led to reckless behaviour.

The risk that is worth taking, if one wishes to live a life gambling-addiction free is, just as Sarah says, getting on with life.

In Group, Sarah has identified the triggers for her gambling addiction, and through her relationships with me as Group therapist and her peer members, she has practised life skills she will need to make changes. Outside of Group, she has built a healthy routine and is actioning change to remove the intensity of triggers for gambling. Women's Group gave her confidence to reduce her gambling; gambling-free time gave her clarity of thought and the ability to manage life better. A better managed life means fewer triggers to gamble. It creates a positive cycle. It is, of course, early on in Sarah's life after Women's Group, but all the good signs are there for her to continue with a healthy recovery.

Cath attended Women's Group meetings with me in a Group that closed after one year in 2011. Here is what she has agreed to share with us from an interview that she recorded herself at home and then sent to me. She was asked to reflect on how things were for her one year after Group closure. This is a verbatim transcript:

> *I was a bit suspicious about going into Women's Group because I didn't talk about my feelings much, but what made the difference for me was that Liz said that I was 'invited' so it made me feel that there was no pressure and that she wouldn't have invited me if she didn't feel I was ready. It felt special somehow, like she wasn't taking women 'willy nilly' just to get bums on seats. Anyway, I really enjoyed my time and learnt a lot about me. For example, I already knew from my one-to-one sessions with Liz that I had a tendency to put other people before me, every time. In Women's Group we could see it happening, I would be in there with advice for everyone else, or cracking a joke to ease the tension and avoid my feelings. I've still got my sense of humour, don't get me wrong! But I learned in Group not to use it to shut my feelings out and to let others have theirs too. One thing I really learned was how to care about others still, but care about myself enough not to take on problems for the world and his wife. That's what got me into trouble with gambling on the laptop in the first place, I would do anything and everything for everyone, and then feel so stressed and worried that I'd gamble to forget my own problems and theirs! Anyway, I was sad that Women's Group was ending but quite philosophical too, that it was a great experience and I had taken so much from it, I felt ready to move on. Since Group started I'd got myself a paid job again and some voluntary work in a charity shop. Actually, it started off as a part of*

> my community service after my court case for theft from work to get money to gamble, but I enjoyed it so much, I stayed on. I love meeting new people now I'm not hiding away feeling guilty and ashamed about gambling and the mess it got me into. Women's Group helped with that, too, because there were other women there who were gambling because they'd been abused and it helped me to understand that another reason I was gambling was to shut out feeling sad about being beaten up for three years by my idiot ex, because when I felt sad I felt weak and I was scared of that feeling. I'd promised myself I would never show weakness again, look where it got me. I know I'd looked at that with Liz in our one-to-one, but hearing other women who felt the same really brought it home. I am still gambling free, I hardly think of it and when I do I don't feel I want to do it. I know you can never say never, but I hope that if I was ever stupid enough to be tempted I'd look at what I've got and think do I really want to risk all this? Before my one-to-one sessions and Women's Group, life was all about work, running round after other people and then gambling to get away from other people. It was like I had a big bag with me and I'd put everyone else's problems in there and carry them round. Now I think I've just about got a balance and have even been on a holiday abroad with the new boyfriend, but I know I'll need to keep my eye on it. But I hope now that if I was ever tempted to gamble again, like I said I'd look at what I've got to lose now and think I'd be mad to risk losing it.
>
> Cath (49 years old, gambling online for five years)

As Cath emphasises, to have something to lose is absolutely a key to remaining free of gambling addiction. Recovery is hard work and as time goes on will become easier, but for all of us when life becomes challenging and we are fearful we operate on lightening-speed, instinctive responses and are in danger of returning to our old favourite from the 'fight, flight or freeze' list. If a woman has invested time and energy in growing a good, rich, abundant life, even if a slip does occur it does not have to mean full-blown relapse, and it is much less likely to result in this if she has much to lose other than money. Let us always remember, gambling addiction was never about winning money, but about feeling there was so little in life to lose it was worth the risk of avoiding the reality of life at all costs.

The woman who at one year follow up is more likely to report that gambling has become problematic for her again, might have become complacent and imagine now that because she has dug out gambling addiction from her life, that it is 'job done' and with no maintenance work she may rest knowing it will never return. My experience is that this very rarely happens; most women after Women's Group understand well that there are always *reasons* for the growth of gambling addiction and that these need to be addressed to keep the problem at bay. More often, relapse might be because a woman has focused more on merely trying to keep the weeds of addiction from growing, but kept a barren and bland life garden of her life, where there has been much time, space and opportunity for gambling to get a grip on her once again. This is not through laziness or complacency but often once again through fear. If throughout her time in Women's Group she has used the experience as a place to take the edge off her need for company and not practised developing relationships in her world outside of Group she is more vulnerable to relapse to gambling as a continued suppression for feelings that still have no avenue of expression through contact with others.

As we discussed earlier, for a very few women what might outweigh their fear of relapse is their fear of being left alone and lonely if they break the rules of 'Don't be well' or 'Don't grow up'. Often, such women are those whose trust has been most deeply damaged and have a deeply rooted belief that their needs will only be met if they remain 'ill' with gambling addiction, or in a childlike dependent state, unable to cope with life. Sadly, the roots of these beliefs run much deeper than the roots of gambling addiction and, if not removed, will leave room for gambling to begin to run rife once again as this childlike and overly dependent state does not bring her either happiness or the care at the level that she so deeply longs for. Gambling addiction grows again as a salve for her fear and loneliness and as a pleading scream from her inner Child to be rescued, if she has given up hope of her Adult voice being heard and taken seriously when she asks for help. Rebecca has kindly agreed to share with us her recorded interview reflecting on her experience of her first year after a 2012 Women's Group to illustrate these themes:

> *I knew I didn't feel ready to leave Women's Group when the year was up. I had worked really hard to behave like an adult in Group, when I first started I wouldn't look at Liz or the other women, I would just sit silent and with my arms folded to try to get attention. Liz helped me to see that my behaviour was speaking volumes. When I was growing up in my family as the youngest one of six kids, mum would always tell me that the others were cleverer or prettier than me and I wouldn't get any attention unless I was being naughty, I always felt left out. Liz helped me to see that I was just repeating*

that in Women's Group, I was scared of feeling left out by the other women and so behaved badly to get attention, but all it did was drive people away from me. That's what I was doing everywhere in my life. In Group they wouldn't let me get away with it, in the nicest way they made me behave like a grown up and Liz encouraged me to get my voice heard instead of acting out. I started to grow up and to hate feeling or being treated like a child, in or out of Group. I'd been so low at times before Group I'd made three suicide attempts and been diagnosed with depression and all sorts and ended up in and out of the mental health system. I started gambling to try to help me forget about feeling lonely and miserable. Also, I would use gambling instead of medication sometimes, because what the psychiatrist gave me would sometimes leave me feeling physically sick and like I couldn't function, so I would take myself off the medication and gamble to feel better instead. I was doing really well for a bit, but struggled to make friends outside of Group, because to be honest I spent most of my time either on my own or with my family wishing I could put things right. When Women's Group ended I was scared but thought I would be okay. I had always hoped that one day my family would see how well I'd done and be proud of me, but it seemed that the better I got the less they bothered with me. Mental health services thought I was doing really well and so stopped my care coordinator. I guess somewhere inside of me I started thinking 'what's the point?' At least when I was gambling people worried about me and noticed me more. I started to get cravings to gamble again because I was so miserable and hated my life, so I just gave in. I regret it now, because believe it or not I do want my life to be different. It's like I want change, but I'm scared of it, because it's either stay with mental health system and my crap family or sit alone, with my only friend being a fruit machine. I am just going to have to be brave and go out there and get a life and meet new people if I want it to happen.

(Rebecca, 28 years old, gambling on
slot machines for eight years)

When I first began to practise in the area of problem gambling in 2001 a strategy for relapse prevention that would be offered by my colleagues and myself would be to avoid walking past the favourite bookmakers or the arcade (now 'adult gaming centre', as they are referred to in the UK) and to rebuild a social life that had perhaps included friends who gambled. The idea of course was to make efforts to avoid as far as possible any images, sights and sounds that might lead to temptation or trigger cravings to gamble. One thing peculiar to gambling more than addiction to drugs or to alcohol, and that I believe is one of the reasons recovery from gambling addiction is notoriously hard, is that so much of that which is addictive exists in the mind. It is about connection to images on a screen, which then become so ingrained as the addiction takes hold that they exist on the video screen playing in the mind of the woman obsessed by them, a constant reminder and invitation to her alternative reality that sucks her in to the game and out of the reality she is struggling to cope with. Many women have shared with me and with Women's Group that they are haunted by the images and sounds associated with their gambling, even when not actively engaged in playing. During recovery from gambling so much as a sound reminiscent to that of a slot machine or a TV advertisement for a gambling game can be enough to trigger the familiar and feared longing for the soothing effects that she knows she would experience whilst playing, even though she rationally knows it will be followed by regret and remorse and days of inner battling her cravings to stay and play. Since the Gambling Act 2007, the gambling industry has been able to freely advertise their products provided that they are deemed not to be targeting the vulnerable.

According to Ofcom, the number of gambling-related advertisements on UK television has multiplied by six since deregulation (Gambling Compliance, 2013). In 2012 the figures were:

- Almost 14 million gambling advertisements ran in the UK compared with 234,000 in 2007.
- Bingo has the most TV advertisements at 532,000.
- Online casino and poker ran 411,000 advertisements.
- Lottery and scratchcards ran 355,000 advertisements.
- Almost 30 per cent of all TV gambling advertisements were for online casino and poker.

Women in recovery from gambling addiction are extremely vulnerable to relapse, and the prevalence of advertising on television, and of pop-ups on computers and Smartphones on occasion dropping into their mailbox – emailed invitations to come back and play, which in some cases might include a gift of cash in their gambling account – all make it impossible to avoid opportunities to gamble if one is going to engage in the modern and ever more technological world. In saying this, I do not wish it to be heard as pointing the finger of accusation at the gambling industry for behaving in a way that is irresponsible or deliberately wishing to create problem gamblers. For the vast majority of those of us who gamble, it will remain a healthy source of entertainment and escapism, as Patrick Basham puts forward in his book *Gambling: A Healthy Bet* (Basham & Luik, 2011). There is, I believe, no statistical evidence to suggest that an increase in advertising has created an increase in women with gambling addiction and anecdotally I have no evidence to suggest that might be so. As I put forward throughout this book and emphasise in Chapter 1, the evidence of my clinical practice is that gambling addiction in women is a mental health problem and a social problem. What I do hear and see to be the facts of the impact of advertising on the woman in *recovery* from gambling addiction is that the images, sights and sounds can frequently be painful reminders of that which she is rationally wanting to recover from, to 'get over', but at times she will still long for. An analogy that we might all be able to relate to, to some degree, is trying to 'get over' a painful break-up, to recover from a broken heart. Recovery from gambling addiction is a similar sensation of having something that feels still very much a part of you wrenched away. That sickening, hollow feeling of being unable to believe that it would be possible to tolerate any greater emotional pain and psychological torture at missing and craving the longed-for love, the being unable to imagine that you will ever recover from those feelings. I imagine that most of us reading this will be able to empathise in some way with those feelings and, if so, then we can empathise a little with what it feels like for the woman in recovery from gambling addiction. Imagine now going through that break-up surrounded by images of your ex, photos, and even videos, of the ex you are trying to get over; their image, their voice coming into your home where you are trying to comfort yourself and move on. That is as close as we might come to experiencing the effect of gambling advertising, at its current level, on the woman in recovery. One effect is to perpetuate the cycle of fear-driven escapism, with her running faster and faster and running out of safe places to hide. Veronica, who worked with me in Women's Group for Problem Gambling, which closed in 2011, describes this well:

> *I sometimes experience flashbacks from the sexual abuse I experienced as a child. I used to self-harm, cut myself, burn myself, to focus on the physical pain was better than the flashbacks, because when they came I would feel just like I was back there, in the abuse. Then I started gambling online, it would help me to block out the urges to harm myself when the flashbacks came. I got myself into financial trouble gambling too much, so had counselling for gambling in one-to-one and Women's Group. One way I learned to cope*

better was to put on the TV and watch comedy or light entertainment to help me to forget about gambling urges and self-harm when flashbacks came, but now the gambling advertisements are everywhere. Even if I wasn't thinking about gambling, by the time I've watched half an hour's TV I am! I also like going to live TV show recordings, it's a way for me to get out and socialise with friends and meet new like-minded people. They just sent me an invitation to the recording of a live gambling show, where the audience would participate in gambling. Women who accepted the invitation were being offered free drinks. You can't get away from it.

(Veronica, gambling for eight years on slot machines and online, 45 years old)

So, when we can no longer cross the road to avoid the AGC, then what is the answer? What strategy can we put in place? Perhaps there is none. The ever resourceful Veronica took to watching her favourite TV programmes on catch up and opened a new email account so that if they arrived, she could avoid seeing invitations from gambling sites she had left. She described feeling resentful at having to narrow down her life to avoid gambling advertisements at a time when she wanted to expand her world view. What this exploration of gambling advertising does emphasise is the vital importance of doing as much therapeutic work in Women's Group as possible to identify what it is, in situations, thoughts and feelings that triggers gambling. Women's Group, as we have seen, is a rich source of all of these triggers with the opportunity for such varied relational dynamics, so many situations replicating life and its losses, attachments and separations. The importance we see again of these things that in a woman's inner or outer world cause her such distress having being resolved, where there cannot be healthy practical resolution, when emotions in a particular area might always be tender, triggers might be avoided. It is equally vital that she has healthy forms of comfort, escapism and adequate support for when life gets tough. It makes sense, if we relate it again to the bad relationship break up; are we not all much less likely to go back to the destructive relationship with the ex, no matter how many reminders they might send, if life is good? Really, it is much the same with gambling addiction.

By the time Women's Group closes at one year, if the process has worked well and they have worked hard to look in the metaphorical mirror at their gambling addiction in relation to themselves and their lives, the vast majority of women will be beyond wanting or needing practical strategies to stop or control their gambling. Relapse prevention is covered constantly by the very process as it is of course the essence of Women's Group as a woman works towards her healthier intrapersonal and so interpersonal relationship and so eventually ending her relationship with gambling addiction. As closure approaches, she may become concerned or keen to have advice and suggestions as to what she might do if relapse does occur. She might be just as keen for suggestions as to which organisations she might contact to progress with her self-development and to continue to grow a rich and fulfilling life. This of course is all to be encouraged, always remembering that Women's Group for Problem Gambling is all about thoughts, feelings and *action*. The list below offers suggestions based on what has proved through experience, of all Women's Groups I have worked with so far, to be helpful.

If relapse occurs:

- Put distance between you and the environment you gambled in, whether the AGM or the computer or your Smartphone. If you have had a relapse you will be vulnerable to feeling you want to gamble again for a while after.
- Do not beat yourself up. Punishing yourself in any way for gambling will only make you feel even worse. The worse you feel, the more likely you are to want to gamble again.
- If you do not feel you can trust yourself to stay away from gambling at the moment, maybe think about taking the pressure off by asking someone you can trust to take care of your cards and cash for a while. Maybe think about self-exclusion from the AGM or from the online gambling site.
- Remember that suppression of feelings drives gambling, expression of feelings helps stop it. As soon as possible contact someone you can trust to talk to about what happened and how you feel now.
- Treat yourself like you would your own best friend if they had just had a shock. You will feel upset and shaken by a relapse. Slow down, comfort yourself, do something soothing – take a bath, watch a movie.
- Once things have settled for you, take a little time to reflect on what happened. Relapse can be a message that things are not okay in life. Ask yourself, has something changed at home? At work? In your relationships? Before you gambled, were you thinking or feeling something you did not feel comfortable with?
- Think about your time in Women's Group and what you learned about yourself. What kinds of situations trigger gambling urges for you? What kind of thoughts? What kind of feelings? What did you learn you can do to help yourself to feel safe? How can you comfort

yourself? How can you let out your anger? How can you express your thoughts and feelings better?
- If you feel at risk of gambling again, or are feeling very vulnerable, it is okay to seek further professional help. Relapse is normal and can happen at any stage of recovery.

Some women may feel reassured by the awareness of agencies to contact if relapse does occur. Also, women do occasionally need additional or specialist support for issues that have been flagged up as a result of the Women's Group process, and they may need more time and attention than it is possible to provide within the process of Group. Women's Group for Problem Gambling is, as we have seen, a place to bring the *whole* of one, as a holistic approach is, in the findings of my practice, a very effective treatment model. Many women who have attended Women's Group over the years, just like Paula and Helen, have had experience of their self being divided up for treatment – being treated for their addiction here, for their depression there, their anxiety elsewhere – and it has not proved successful for them, as to effectively treat the addiction their gambling needed to be seen as self-medication for the depression and anxiety, and their depression and anxiety as a symptom of underlying issues perhaps in awareness or lying buried away where it was hoped they would never have to see the light of day. There may be times for a woman when the result of trusting enough to be increasingly open with herself and with others means that light is shed on an issue that feels for her so sensitive or so terrifying that she is aware that it might be unproductive, or potentially even dangerous, for her to do more than put a metaphorical label on the box that she has now discovered it lies in and make a decision to unpack it in an environment where she feels safe and confident to do so. Remember, for example, Helen's identifying that her unresolved issues around her rape trauma were constantly troubling her and driving her addiction to gambling. She was aware that the issues attached to this felt potentially overwhelming without adequate support outside of Women's Group and that she needed to give exclusive attention to them in a specialised group. What feels too much to unpack in Women's Group for Problem Gambling will vary from woman to woman and will depend on each woman's own psychology and emotional resilience and life experience, and of course the particular dynamics of her Group. Again I would wish to emphasise that the ideal is that she is encouraged to be increasingly open and to face the truth within herself and about her life situation, however the important factor is that she is encouraged and not discouraged by being pushed to reveal more than she is ready to. She has been defending herself against reality for very good reason. If she has the feeling that her defences are being smashed down, she will build them even higher and stronger and this in itself may cause a backward slide regarding her gambling addiction as a cornerstone of defensive behaviour. If she is allowed to work at her own pace, she is much more likely to become less defensive. Part of the purpose of Women's Group is to act as a mirror to reflect to her what it is that needs to change and as a practice ground for beginning that process of change. Some women may complete their desired process of change, and complete their personal agenda within the life of Women's Group; and some may find that they need a little more time, a little extra support, or support of a different kind, or as Helen did, to discover that their personal agenda of understanding why their gambling addiction took hold was a larger and more challenging issue than they had realised. The changes a woman needs to make may take time, and she needs to be given every encouragement and the message that it is not a failing if she needs to move on to further support at Women's Group closure. Indeed, rather than this being a sign of either her failure or that of Women's Group, the fact that she now sees being able to ask for her needs to be met and to trust enough to depend on others to support her is a testament to just how far she has come from the other side of the spectrum where she existed in relative isolation, repeating her mantra 'Don't be close'.

Below is a list that has so far proved valuable throughout my practice for women who request referrals during Women's Group, or at closure:

Citizens Advice

Helping people to resolve their legal, money and other problems by providing free, independent and confidential advice.

www.citizensadvice.org.uk

T: 08444 111 444 (UK)

GamCare

Support, information and advice to anyone suffering from a gambling problem.

www.gamcare.org.uk

Helpline: 0808 8020 133

Gordon Moody Association

Specialist support and treatment for acutely addicted gamblers.

www.gordonmoody.org.uk

T: 01384 241292

Mind

Advice and support for anyone with a mental health problem.

www.mind.org.uk

T: 0300 123 3393

Money Advice Service

Free, independent financial advice.

www.moneyadviceservice.org.uk

T: 0300 500 5000

National Problem Gambling Clinic

Treating problem gamblers, their partners and family members in England and Wales.

www.cnwl.nhs.uk/cnwl-national-problem-gambling-clinic/

T: 020 7534 6699

NSPCC Adults Abused in Childhood

Advice and support from our helpline for adult survivors of child abuse and neglect.

www.nspcc.org.uk

Helpline 0808 800 5000 (24 hrs, 7 days per week)

Rape Crisis. England and Wales

Confidential helpline, face-to-face support or counselling.

Freephone: 0808 802 9999

Refuge

Help for women and children who have experienced domestic violence.

www.refuge.org.uk

Helpline: 0808 2000 247

Relate

Offers relationship counselling, sex therapy, workshops, mediation, consultations, support. Face to face, by telephone and online.

www.relate.org.uk

T: 0300 100 1234

Samaritans

Confidential emotional support 24/7.

www.samaritans.org

Helpline: 0845 7909 090

Chapter 7

For the practitioner
Starting Women's Group for Problem Gambling

Women with gambling addiction are notoriously hard to engage in treatment and have a high rate of attrition. For anyone who has now read this book and perhaps *Women and Problem Gambling* (Karter, 2013), you will by now have an understanding of why this is so. To summarise, gambling to a woman is a true dependency. Despite the destruction it will ultimately bring upon her inner and outer world, her intrapersonal and interpersonal relationships, she has now got herself caught in a trap; when she first began gambling for escapism, absorption in the gambling activity did help her to feel more psychologically in control and therefore of course emotionally so. At some point, unaffordable amounts of time spent gambling meant that she paid no attention to the problems she was attempting to avoid and so they at best remain as intolerable as she perceived them to be when she became vulnerable to addiction to block them out, and at worse they have become magnified into even bigger and more terrifying monsters, which she is still running from. Unaffordable amounts of money spent triggered a cycle of loss chasing, each new loss feeling more painful and depressing.

> *Every time I lose, it's like a knife through me . . .*
> (Carina, gambling on casino slot machines for 15 years, 50 years old)

She is likely to have a mountain of debt, credit cards, payday loans, money borrowed, or perhaps stolen from friends and family. Hanging on to the tiny hope that she just might still win her way out of the ever tightening trap, that she might just have the money to pay back that payday loan on time, but knowing deep within herself that that will not happen and that any money won will just enable her to stay and play. By now each day the world seems more a battleground.

. . . I feel I'm at war with everyone.

(Carina)

If she is still to any extent regularly gambling, she knows that to stop will be her biggest and fiercest battle yet: the battle with the pain and depression of withdrawal, the separation from and loss of that which has perhaps been her strongest, perhaps her only, attachment. We know too that the result of her life experiences until now, combined with the consequences of gambling addiction and its related issues, leave her self-esteem in shreds. Even if she has managed so far to control or even to stop her gambling behaviour, to make her way so far down the path of recovery to the very first Women's Group meeting, she has to find enough strength to make that journey despite carrying with her feelings of guilt, shame, fear of rejection, fear of judgement, fear of uncertainty. Fear of attachment, separation and loss (Bowlby, 1986). To encourage herself to come to Women's Group, despite her fear of being close with others because of all that life has taught her, she will risk in intimate relationship. A big risk too, if a paradoxical one, is that the therapy might actually work. What we most want is often what we most fear and when at that stage of the process all she knows is that, as much as she despises it, she depends on her addiction to get her through, there will be a high level of ambivalence to letting go. Letting go of gambling means change, change means a degree of uncertainty, and uncertainty means fear. She responds to fear by taking flight from the thought of treatment; or by freezing with fear and so being unable to make the decision of whether to engage in treatment or to retreat to the painful but familiar life of addiction; or perhaps by going into fight and finding 101 pieces of evidence for why that therapist or that treatment organisation just cannot be trusted, so she should not engage further than assessment.

So what makes the difference in her decision as to whether she decides to engage further than the first telephone call or email enquiring about Women's Group meetings, let alone the assessment process? The findings of my practice are that there is no rocket science required for this, any more than there is for getting to the roots of her addiction. Those of us who are Women's Group therapists need to start as we mean to go on and from the very first point of contact make our focus that of building a healthy relationship, which just so happens also to be a therapeutic one. By this I am not suggesting that we are overly or inappropriately friendly, of course we must at all times adhere to ethics, the guidelines, policies and procedures of our professional bodies and treatment agencies we are employed by. In fact to cross boundaries might initially be as off-putting to the woman seeking treatment as a colder, clinical approach. Let us remember that we are often relating to women who have histories of abuse and it may be particularly important and encouraging for them to see that we are boundaried. What I am strongly suggesting is that we demonstrate warmth and humanity from the very first point of contact, and find some way of engaging with the woman who is approaching us as an individual, not just as a 'gambler'. At the same time, however, communicating in any way possible, and as soon as possible, we do have an understanding of the particular issues that come with gambling addiction. Women with gambling addiction are very much aware that their addiction, while similar in some ways to substance misuse, can be even more complex and has distinct differences. They are encouraged and reassured to hear that they would be working with someone who understands their issues. I would suggest from my experience that we cannot do this well hiding behind a clipboard at assessment, when a woman is aware that we are more focused on ticking boxes that on getting to know her.

A woman coming to Women's Group is likely to be someone who already has had some counselling or therapy and so may be expecting a little form filling. Of course we do live in an age where we need to collect data not only for client safety and case formulation, but also in some cases for reasons of securing funding and monitoring our success rates to ensure we are providing the best standard of care to our clients. It is in the way that we do this, however, that will make the difference as to whether we encourage or discourage a potential Women's Group member to attend that very first Group meeting. If we are to engage her it is vital to remember that in assessment it is not only crucial that we get a sense of her, to assess whether Group will be appropriate for her, and that it will be appropriate for Women's Group that she attend, but she also gets a sense of us as Women's Group therapist. If we can create a sense of safe engagement in that meeting she is much more likely to commit to Women's Group meetings than if we present as a detached clinician intent on form filling and box ticking. In my experience there is little that has sparked more annoyance and frustration, more mistrust and more decisions to bolt for the door, than the latter behaviour as I have heard it reported by clients throughout my professional career. We are meeting women who are very often likely to have had negative experiences of authority and inappropriate use of power and control. They are also suspicious perhaps of mental health settings; many women speak of their experience of the psychiatric setting as feeling made to fit into a box, of being a diagnosis rather than a person, and found this objectifying. Coming to be assessed as a 'gambler' may feel much the same and with additional concerns for what might happen with any information gathered and the consequences of this for any mental health service involvement, social service involvement if she has children, or indeed legal ramifications if she has committed illegal acts, and so transparency is essential. Be careful to outline the purpose of asking the questions and what will happen after the assessment to the information she gives. I would emphasise that I am always careful to assure each woman who is coming into Women's Group that what she has shared with me in any one-to-one sessions we have had together, or in assessment she has shared with me alone (including of course any limits to confidentiality such as clinical supervision), that I will not share what she had told me in any Women's Group meeting unless she raises an issue herself and makes it clear to Group that I already know what she is now sharing with them. It takes time for trust to build in the group process and so what she may feel comfortable with telling me she may not yet be ready to share with others. Knowing I will keep her confidence removes the fear of my disclosing her secrets as a barrier to entering Group.

When I am assessing a woman as a potential Women's Group member, whether we have met before in a one-to-one setting or it is our first meeting, I will meet her face to face for 50 minutes during which time I will ask the questions I need to ask in as an informal way as possible, with my focus always being on what experience has proved to me will encourage her to take the next step of coming to that first Group meeting, the beginnings of building a trusted *relationship*. Depending on the setting in which we are working there will of course be differing requirements for data collection. The Women's Groups for Problem Gambling, which I now facilitate, take place through my private practice, Level Ground, and so I am able to use questions that to me have proved important in assessing whether Women's Group will be of value to a woman, and whether she will be of value to the Group and, on occasion, these might be two different things. On the very rare occasion I have met with women, frequently with a mental health diagnosis of borderline personality disorder, whose particularly damaging pasts have meant that their needs for care and attention have been so great that sadly the effects of being present in the Group meeting would bring up an intensity of transferential responses such as to mean that Women's Group for Problem Gambling would be inappropriate and, at worst, unsafe for them. For Women's Group as a whole, the impact of the woman's particular depth of needs is likely to be detrimental and perhaps cause an increase in missed meetings or women leaving Group. For the woman who has such a high level of needs, her needs are often beyond the limitations of Women's Group space and time to work through and it would be better, where possible, to make an appropriate referral to a more appropriate treatment service.

It is very important to bear in mind what I have just said above, that not every woman will benefit from Women's Group, or Women's Group benefit from her membership. When considering inviting women to Group, I have found that having a wide range, in terms of age, socioeconomic background and cultural and religious background, helps to create the sense of Women's Group being a microcosm of the wider world and so is valuable. Cultural and religious diversity may of course vary depending on the area in which Women's Group meets. I have found that Groups in London have a greater ethnic and religious diversity than Women's Group meetings in Sussex, where I have met a higher proportion of women who are bisexual or lesbian. Each area might present issues that may contribute to gambling addiction, for example the stress, anxiety and loneliness of inner city life, or the stress and anxiety of family and friends who are rejecting and judging of a woman's sexuality.

It is fair on both the individual and the Group to be careful to discern who to invite into any Group, therefore, as well as ascertaining the stage at which they are, currently, in their recovery from gambling addiction, I am interested particularly in the experiences that potential Women's Group members have had in family groups, other social groups or therapeutic groups as it will help me to gauge how they might respond transferentially to the Women's Group process.

Assessment questions for Women's Group for Problem Gambling

- What was your position in your family? Were you the eldest, youngest or middle child?
- How was affection demonstrated in your family?
- How did you perceive conflict resolved within your family?
- If you were to describe your family's own set of rules, what would you say they were?
- How was your relationship with your mother?
- How was your relationship with your father?
- What is your unhappiest memory of family?
- What is your happiest memory of family?

- At school did you make friends easily?
- Were you more inclined to have one close friend at school, or mix in groups of several friends?
- How was your relationship with your teachers?
- What is your unhappiest memory of school?
- What is your happiest memory of school?
- Did you attend any after school clubs?

- In the work place, do you tend to make friends?
- Do you like to work alone, or do you like to feel part of a team?
- How would you describe your relationship with your boss or management?
- What is your unhappiest workplace memory?
- What is your happiest workplace memory?

- Do you belong to any religious faith groups?
- Are you a member of any social clubs or social groups?

- Have you ever attended any Anonymous meetings (such as Gamblers Anonymous?) or any therapeutic groups or groups provided by mental health services?
- If you have attended any Anonymous meetings or any peer support or therapeutic groups:
   - Did you attend voluntarily?
   - What did you find most helpful about them?
   - What was most unhelpful?
   - If you left the group prematurely, what prompted that?

Depending on the therapeutic setting and requirements for problem gambling and mental health screening, the questions above or an extracted variation of them, can be used instead of, or as well as, screens for problem gambling such as the screen that I use, which is the DSM-IV (American Psychiatric Association (APA), 2005). The recently published DSM-5 (APA, 2013) has re-classified gambling from an impulse control disorder to an addiction, which certainly fits with the experience of the women with whom I work and my sense of the problem as a clinician. If I know of a potential Women's Group member's pattern of gambling because she and I have worked, or perhaps still are working together, in one-to-one work, it is useful to ascertain her gambling pattern before Women's Group starts and at its closure when I again use the DSM-IV, in order to monitor both the effectiveness of that particular Women's Group and the individual progress of each Group member; it can be confidence inspiring to have 'on paper' a record that, for example, by the end of Women's Group a woman is no longer preoccupied with gambling or using it for escape from intolerable thoughts and feelings. The repetition of the questions regarding the happiest and unhappiest memories is aimed at highlighting what might be any particular flashpoints for transference within Women's Group. This may help not only the therapist to know what dynamics potentially to expect in Group, but might inform the new Group member what she might like her personal agenda for the Group process to be. If, for example, her unhappiest memories are of feeling excluded – as we might remember with Terri's struggle within the Women's Group that we followed – her personal agenda might be to work towards including herself more actively in relationships developing within the Group process, thus giving herself fresh evidence that now, as an adult, she can be part of a group and not always suffer those horrible feelings of being left out of family intimacies, or of the playtime games at school. Asking about her relationship with her parents, her teachers and her boss in the workplace will help to gauge her expectations of her relationship with the Group therapist, who transferentially is viewed as an authority figure. This is all valuable information, which must somehow be absorbed by the Group therapist but not disclosed in Women's Group meetings unless disclosed by the woman concerned. You may be thinking that this is a tricky task and indeed you are right and one requiring very good memory of what she has said when and to whom. Good note-taking can aid in remembering the setting in which any information was disclosed and it is very worthwhile making the effort. Any indiscreet disclosure by the therapist can deeply damage the trust between the therapist and the Group member it concerns and indeed between the therapist and the rest of Women's Group who witness this.

You may of course choose not to, or your work setting may not allow you to, work in one-to-one therapy as well as in the Group setting with Women's Group members. You may choose not to, or your work settings may not permit you to, assess the potential Women's Group members with whom you will work. Having had experiences of both conducting assessments myself of potential Women's Group members, and having assessments conducted by another therapist in the agency setting within which I have worked, I recommend if at all possible that Women's Group therapists conduct assessment themselves. The attendance rates for new Group members at their first Women's Group meetings are significantly very much higher for women whom I have assessed myself, regardless of whether they have previously worked with me in one-to-one therapy, than they are if the assessment has been conducted by another clinician. Within my own practice, and taking into consideration assessments that I have conducted for other agencies where I have set up and facilitated Women's Groups for Problem Gambling, and using their screening process, just under 90 per cent of the women I have myself assessed as finding Women's Group to be of value to them, have then attended the Women's Group meetings. I believe this to be for the reason we have highlighted again and again in this book and that it is because *it really is all about relationship*. If a woman meets in assessment with the therapist with whom she will work she at least has the start of one attachment, one familiar face, and one person in whom to begin to rebuild her shattered trust in human attachment. If the questions I have suggested for assessment have been put forward in conversational style during the assessment meeting she will in all likelihood have begun to open up and to express. Let us remember always that assessment is a two-way process and if she has been able to see from your responses that you remain unshaken and yet empathic and understanding of the complexities and dire consequences of her gambling addiction, it will encourage her to take that step over the threshold of her very first Group meeting.

After assessment, keeping the as yet tenuous attachment strong is of value in encouraging her attendance. A text or email reminder of the date, time and address of the first meeting serves two purposes; it maintains engagement and a sense of trusted relationship and provides a genuinely valuable reminder of when the meeting will take place. I respect that some schools of therapeutic thought would advocate leaving it as the client's responsibility to remember meetings, as a part of the woman's recovery process is to begin to take responsibility for her actions. I believe, however, through the findings of my practice this contact and reminder to be helpful because she is battling with gambling addiction. Her addiction, to a high degree, has been about disengaging with relationships and with life, and its overwhelming responsibilities and a part of the harsh consequences have meant both practical chaos and chaotic thinking. A missed meeting or late arrival might mean that she has an understandable level of ambivalence or wish to avoid what she will see reflected in the crystal clear Women's Group mirror, or it might genuinely mean that there has been a lost Women's Group invitation, or that the years of chaos in a life lived in cyber space or in front of the screen of the slot machine, have resulted in it feeling hard to begin to create a frame of routine and ritual and literally to hold in mind or open that piece of paper with the details of the first Group meeting. It can be that the time between assessment and the start of

Women's Group has allowed dark projections based on past relationship horrors to create 101 reasons she should not attend, which a brief text or email could help her dispel by reminding her that her Women's Group therapist actually did not seem the same as her parents, her teachers, her boss; it reminds her of a satisfactory first meeting with her therapist in assessment, when for an hour she felt she just might be able to trust enough to give a meeting a go. . . . Yes, I would certainly agree that she needs to begin to take on the responsibilities connected with being an individual and part of the wider community, and that is exactly what Women's Group is about. No work can be done, however, unless a woman is in that very first Women's Group meeting. I strongly suggest doing all that is possible in an appropriate and ethical way to encourage her through holding that delicate thread of relationship that now connects her with the Group therapist and so leads her to Women's Group. Another way of reinforcing this connection is by sending regular reminders of Women's Group meetings, cancellations owing to therapist illness, or late starting of a meeting via an inclusive Group text message addressed to the whole Group, perhaps using a term that they might have adopted to describe themselves as a Group. As we heard, Sarah referred to her Group as 'the girls', which was a term this Women's Group used to describe themselves, so my text might be addressed to 'Women's Group Girls', or 'Women's Group Ladies', as many Groups have chosen to address themselves. This may seem like a small and relatively insignificant detail, but if we remind ourselves that we are working with women who have good reason to avoid intimacy, and for whom gambling addiction has made this possibility even more remote, such a text creates a sense of belonging to a community and is a reminder of their importance of the responsibility they have towards each other to create and keep their Women's Group alive. As I often remind the Group, each individual within it creates the life of Women's Group; without their attendance and input, it would not exist.

Once in that meeting, during the first session it is important to draw up a contract to work together. This might be on paper or it might be a verbal contract, whichever is more appropriate to the setting and practice style. I have found that in most Women's Group meetings the preference is for a verbal contract and this has proven to be adequate. As we have discussed, there tends to be a general sense of distrust and a feeling of being disheartened with bureaucracy, and too much form filling has the effect of feeling objectified and driving a wedge in the precious process of person-to-person relating.

> **Essential areas to cover in a Women's Group for Problem Gambling contract:**
> - Duration of Women's Group
> - Confidentiality and its limitations
> - Donations/fees (where applicable)
> - Punctuality and attendance
> - Who to contact in case of illness or lateness
> - How Women's Group will be informed in case of therapist absence
> - Contact between Women's Group members outside of Women's Group time

Women's Groups for Problem Gambling treats both the symptom of gambling addiction and the underlying cause, the cause being as I here propose from extensive clinical experience to be dysfunctional, distressing and damaging intrapersonal and interpersonal relationship. The duration of each Women's Group that I now facilitate is one year to 18 months. I have made this decision having in the past run both open-ended Women's Groups and shorter term Women's Groups of six months. Having run open-ended Groups, the difficulty was that the Group members, having no deadline for their therapeutic work and for the vital aspect of taking skills outside to build a productive life, might become dependent on Women's Group to shield them from life, as they had with gambling addiction. A positive of having a limit to the time we use in any area of life is that it can cause us to focus our attention on how we use it best. The main difficulty I encountered with shorter term Women's Groups of six months was that it was much more difficult to create the sense of a microcosm of life, for example terms of learning to cope with separation and loss, as it was impractical for these Groups to be open groups, with new members joining up until the six-month period, as in longer term Groups. The attachment aspect equally was an issue because, as we have seen in the Women's Group we have followed, difficulty in developing trust in others is a strong and constant theme for women who attend. It takes time for Group to move on from discussing the safe surface level of gambling addiction to the more uncomfortable depths of facing what fears drive it, to get Group members' trust. I have noticed a definite pattern of Group members naturally both feeling ready, and being ready, to move on from Women's Group at one year to 18 months. This might by contemporary standards seem like a long time in treatment; however, given the issues underlying the gambling addiction, either presenting or unconscious, perhaps this length of time is reasonable, and the finding of my practice is that it is certainly effective. I have found that by the one year to 18 month period 92 per cent of women who have been through the entire Women's Group process from start to finish are gambling free and, key to remaining gambling free, have built healthy and productive lifestyles using the relational skills and life skills they have worked on in Women's Group. Eighty eight per cent have reported remaining gambling free at one year follow up meeting.

Significant reasons for this time frame working so well is that, combined with the relational focused group therapy, it allows for relationships to more fully develop along with all of the ups and downs we must learn to work through if we are to healthily relate. Also within that year a woman will live through and be likely to discuss in Women's Group various meaningful events: birthdays, Christmas, anniversaries of births and deaths, even changes of season, which might affect her mood and so too her gambling urge, thus providing much rich material for her to learn more about herself, what triggers her gambling and how to cope better and work towards life in the next year without it.

It is reassuring to make explicit confidentiality limitations. Shared by women within the Women's Group room are frequent stories of the depths to which gambling addiction has dragged them. We will witness tears of shame and disbelief at the levels to which their behaviour sank as individual women speak of theft, lies told to, and manipulation of, those they care for to get money to gamble or just to scrape by another day of fending off the wolves from their door. We will hear of credit cards taken out in the names of partners, cards and money stolen from family, children left at home alone for trips to the AGC, or left unattended for hours, whilst their mother gambled her way into the oblivion offered by her computer screen. We will hear of women turning to prostitution, theft from work, stealing food from the supermarket to sell or to feed their family when their gambling addiction has swallowed every last penny they possessed. Rates of attempted suicide among gambling addicts are around double the UK national average (NHS, 2013). If a woman knows the limitations to confidentiality, as well as what will stay held within the confidentiality of Women's Group, she will feel safer to confront the truth for herself and to share this with others.

> *I hate myself. My daughter phoned me, she had a call from the credit card company. I took a card in her name without telling her and*

> spent £5000 and never paid it back. She won't talk to me and says she's going to call the police. I don't blame her, I deserve it. I just can't bear that I think she won't speak to me, ever again.
>
> (Marcia, gambling on slot machines for 17 years, 49 years old)

If donations or fees are required for the Women's Group meeting, these are collected in a container placed in the Group room at each meeting. The Women's Groups that I now facilitate are low cost and run on fees that cover the cost of room rental and refreshments only, which the Group members are aware of. It is very rare indeed that I have found upon counting that the total for the week's contribution is less than the amount agreed for each member. Women who attend Group meeting might have been dishonest and untrustworthy as a consequence of their gambling addiction, but in recovery are frequently eager to be honest and find it refreshing to begin to take financial responsibility in this way both for themselves and for the continued life of their Women's Group. On the odd occasion when someone has not contributed their fair share to the collection, in practical terms it has been due to relapse or pinching debt repayment and not having available funds; in analysis it has been often that the woman concerned has been used to being overly dependent on others, not in a healthy way, but rather in a childlike way. Being kept overly dependent on parents has been as damaging in many ways as having rejecting and neglecting parents; in neither case has a woman been given the chance to grow and become her functioning Adult self in the world. In both cases she is now fearful of the external world as her inner world is not as yet developed enough to cope with it. As we discussed earlier on, her gambling addiction has grown because she has not been provided with the opportunity for personal growth, and she may be afraid that she will not be valued and cared for if she stops living life by 'Don't grow up'.

As illustration, Zara described to us in Women's Group how the more she grew independent both of her gambling addiction and her parents, and their strict rules for her living her life as a childlike self controlled by them, the less she felt loved and valued by them. On the last visit to the family home, the door had been opened by her mother, who had coldly said 'Oh, it's you', before slamming the door shut in front of her. We had explored how in being herself the 'you' her mother spoke of, she had always instinctively known risked rejection by her family. The purpose gambling addiction had served was to suppress and squeeze down her authentic self, her own true thoughts, feelings, needs and wants, until she was all but unrecognisable even to herself.

> In Women's Group, Zara found that it was possible for her to be valued as an Adult woman and that she did not need to be childlike and overly dependent on others to gain their care. For Zara, beginning to pay her contribution regularly, instead of depending on the other Group members to carry her, was a part of fulfilling her personal agenda.

Punctuality and regular attendance should always be emphasised as important. Regular lateness and poor attendance disrupts the process of check in and, on a wider scale, interrupts the process of attachment for the entire Group; and for the woman who regularly arrives late or misses meetings, it means that not only does she lose the thread of the themes that are naturally developing and being discussed but she misses out on developing trust and growing attachments. She will therefore find it harder to feel a sense of belonging and so be more at risk of returning to the familiar 'Don't be close' rule and of leaving Women's Group prematurely: again, as we witnessed with Terri, during her Group experience. The more meetings that a woman misses, the harder it feels to return and face the shame and embarrassment of her absence, let alone the deeper issues she must face.

If a Women's Group member is running late or cannot attend I ask that she contact me directly, rather than send a message via another Women's Group member, or if I have worked within an agency, than contacting the agency to pass a message to me. I have found through experience that this direct contact has many times saved a Women's Group member, who might be wavering in her courage to stay in Women's Group, from leaving altogether. After a couple of missed Group sessions I might ask, for example, whether there is anything that is making it feel difficult to get to Women's Group at that time? Or, I might mention that I was aware that there had been a little tension between her and another Group member and was there anything about that which might need to be resolved? Unless there are good, practical reasons for absence, like illness or no babysitter or lack of funds to travel, it is likely that whatever is keeping her away is fear based. In passing a message with another Group member, or another agency member with whom she has no relationship, she is much more likely to be able to hide her fear behind excuses of another stomach bug or having to work late again. If she has the beginnings of a relationship with me, she is more likely to open up enough to tell me that perhaps she is worried that what she felt at the last meeting created urges to gamble, or that she is upset and angry with a fellow Group member but scared of what will happen if she shares that in a meeting. I am more likely to be able to have a hunch about this because I have a relationship with her and see her relating in Women's Group. Here is a precious chance, therefore, to give her courage, to explain this is all a part of the process of Women's Group and therefore too of long-term recovery, to facilitate her coming back into Women's Group and to work on facing those fears, working through what it is that has caused her to take flight, because whatever it is that she feels she cannot face that has caused her to run *from* Group, is likely to have her running *to* gambling in life outside, in order to escape from her thoughts and feelings about it. Here again, the key that is likely to keep her in Women's Group at these vulnerable points, is all about relationship.

To the last point on the contract, having said it is all about relationship, it is all about working on relationships and key skills associated with them while inside Women's Group in order to take them outside, but there is risk if relationships within Group are developed outside of Group time, during the life of a Group. During contracting I say that we do not have hard and fast rules stating that there should be no contact outside of Group time, but I do provoke thought about the potential pitfalls, such as how it might be for Lynne if Laura meets and likes the family of Lynne, who Lynne then wants to complain about in the next meeting? Or, what if two Women's Group members become friends outside of Women's Group meetings and then fall out? How comfortable might they be about attending meetings in future? I also remind everyone that a purpose of the process is to widen the horizon of the world of relationships of all kinds and that taking friendships with other members outside of Group might still be avoiding the risk of learning to develop relationships of all kinds in the world outside. We must always be very careful that Women's Group does not replace the stasis engendered by a gambling addiction. It is vital to a woman's recovery that it is not only about defining and expressing thoughts and feelings, as essential as that is, but that it is also about going beyond being frozen by fear, and about learning to *action*.

If relationships do develop outside of Women's Group, I ask that everyone be open about this within Group and if problems arise to discuss them inside of Women's Group, this way maximising the opportunity to learn more about themselves in relationship and minimising the chance of anyone leaving due to undiscussed, and so often not understood or resolved, issues. Difficulties may arise in even the briefest encounters outside of the meeting time, as we see below:

Joanna had missed three meetings in a row. During her absence at the third meeting, Clara hesitantly shared that she wondered if Joanna was feeling too embarrassed to attend. In the last meeting she attended Joanna spoke of having relapsed due to severe depression and, having gambled all her benefits, had nothing left to eat

> *for the next week except a loaf of bread. After the meeting, whilst leaving the building she had asked Clara if she would let her borrow £15, which, feeling sorry for her, Clara had lent to her. Clara had not mentioned this before, as she had felt guilty about what she felt was shaming Joanna, but was also starting to feel resentful that Joanna had not been back to return her money. Once this issue was within the Group space there was opportunity to work on and resolve it, including encouraging Joanna to return and face both her gambling problem and her shame at having borrowed money and letting Clara down by not repaying her. For Clara it was the chance to look at what had hooked her into 'Please others' when she could ill afford to lend Joanna money and as a result had struggled financially.*

Nothing need mean disaster if it is brought back into Women's Group, where it can be transformed into a learning opportunity for how an interaction fits with a woman's pattern of relationship and, so too, with her pattern of gambling to ease the discomfort caused by that unhealthy pattern of relating.

The only other informal addition to the contract is the rule that we touched on earlier in this book:

> *With the exception of physical illness, however you are feeling, come to Women's Group.*

The above aimed to encourage attendance, despite shame and guilt about relapse to gambling, despite fear of what a woman might say or hear in Women's Group, despite fears of breaking the rules of 'Don't be close', 'Don't tell', 'Be strong', despite everything inside her at times telling her to run and hide, come to Women's Group. Rather than instilling fear of the process by predicting fearful feeling, this can normalise the fact that she will at times wish to be anywhere else other than in Women's' Group and takes care of the risk, if left unspoken, that when she feels uncomfortable emotional responses during or after meetings, that Group is making her 'worse' and so causes her to leave prematurely. In fact I have found that being transparent regarding the purpose of the Women's Group process gives focus and helps to make sense of the confusing and conflicting thoughts and feelings that will be experienced along the way. The list below contains the key points that I explain in the first meeting and will return to when appropriate and encouraging throughout the life of any individual Group. I deliberately avoid the use of therapeutic terminology here, as I do in the language I use within Women's Group, in order to de-mystify the process and in doing so grow more trust in myself and in the Women's Group space.

What members might expect from Women's Group for Problem Gambling

- Most women gamble to escape difficult thoughts and feelings about life and relationship.
- Gambling addiction has made it harder to cope with life and to relate healthily.
- In meetings we will sometimes encounter strong emotional responses both to each other and to what we see reflected in ourselves.
- The familiar way of coping has been to gamble, to avoid uncomfortable thoughts and feeling connected to what we see and hear.
- We are in Women's Group to identify the situations, thoughts and feelings which trigger gambling.
- Part of the process is learning how to face and better cope with these scary thoughts and feelings.
- We will experience how healthy expression with trusted others can help ease uncomfortable thoughts and feelings, instead of gambling to suppress them.
- We will use Women's Group as a safe space to practise life skills and relational skills, to begin to take into a gambling-free life outside of Women's Group.

In order for Women's Group to take place at all, there will need to be a regular venue. Regularity of venue and meeting times are important, as with recovery from gambling addiction creating strong routine and ritual is reassuring, and being attached to life by some routine will help to replace the all consuming sense of attachment to gambling addiction. When we are working frequently with the survivors of childhood abuse or domestic violence this will be doubly reassuring; as we have discussed, uncertainty is one of the biggest fears for women who attend Group meetings and so knowing when and where each meeting will be held is extremely important to them and will contribute significantly to regular attendance and low rates of attrition.

The venue itself is important. It may sound like I am stating the obvious, but a reception area in which to wait for those who might arrive early in bad weather, or on a dark night; a pleasant, quiet meeting room, large enough to accommodate eight comfortable chairs and a small table, with an opening window or air conditioning will all again add to the general sense of each individual, and indeed Women's Group as a whole, being valued and taken seriously. I have worked in some settings where Women's Group has been given any room that might happen to be available at that time each week, been moved at short notice to accommodate other meetings, had no window or air conditioning, or has been so small that the many women who attend with high anxiety and panic attack were put off from attending. While none of these situations were created intentionally by those involved in the decision-making process regarding the setting, these things impact on how seriously and important each woman imagines Women's Group is to those who hold it. If a woman does not feel it is important to those who have invited her to attend, why should it be so to her, when she is likely to be at best ambivalent? Unconsciously, the dynamics of being marginalised, not taken seriously by those she perceives to be in authority, it not being important whether her voice gets heard, living life by the rule of 'Don't be important', the sense of being invisible all play into transference projections, which in the early stage of Women's Group cohesion actually *can* make a vast difference to whether or not Women's Group for Problem Gambling works or not, because of course for it to work, it has to have enough members for it to meet.

When choosing a venue, if it can be discreetly situated with no obvious advertising it as a problem gambling treatment centre, so much the better. The stigma associated with gambling addiction makes women reluctant to be openly attending treatment for gambling addiction. Perhaps especially so for the women we are increasingly seeing in treatment; the professional with a position of responsibility at work will often be fearful of the negative effect on her position in the workplace were her addiction to be discovered with all its associations with her not to be trusted around access to money. When choosing the location of the venue it is worth taking time to consider how close Women's Group venue is to any AGC or other gambling establishment. As we have seen, if the meetings are working well they will at times raise uncomfortable feelings and all of the fears that have sent women running for the refuge offered by gambling. It is not at all unusual to find that a woman in the early stages of recovery, who is anxious about attending meetings, will experience cravings to gamble to manage her feelings just before attending a Women's Group meeting. Equally, if she has had a challenging meeting and has not as yet developed the skill of, and experienced the benefits of, expressing her feelings, she may experience urges to gamble to suppress those feelings. While it is true that if she has strong urges to gamble she may travel miles to do so, or as we have said just switch on the computer, or her Smartphone, it makes avoiding gambling before and after meetings just a little easier if there is not the reminder of an AGC just next door. An amusing moment that I can share to illustrate how this can happen was when a few years ago I set up and facilitated a Women's Group for an agency, who had premises on a busy high street, which had an AGC just a few doors away. Maria, who always brought humour to light even the darkest of situations, shared how after feeling upset following a family argument she had been gambling in the AGC for the hour before the Women's Group meeting. With a cheeky smile Maria said to Group, 'Well, there was a sign in the window saying "Gamble Here". So I did!' (Maria, slot machine and online player for ten years, 32 years old). As we have touched on, humour in Women's Group is never in short supply and if appropriately used is all a healthy part of creating the holistic experience of finding alternative ways to gambling for relieving stress and tension.

Once within the safe container of tight framework and boundaries, both Women's Group therapist and Women's Group members are confident of boundaries being maintained; the general atmosphere once within the Group space tends towards informality and between checking in and checking out a free flow of content takes place. This as we have seen will tend to contain strong themes that are repeated Women's Group to Women's Group. I remain convinced as a result of my practice over many hundreds of hours of meetings and many years of working with women and gambling addiction that despite the recurring themes it is much more valuable to allow these themes to develop naturally as a part of the Group process, rather than to formulate a recovery treatment plan with meetings structured around a particular theme, such as dealing with uncertainty or exploring trust issues. As we saw in earlier chapters, gambling addiction underneath the symptomatic chaos is in actual fact an attempt to be in control of thoughts and feelings triggered by that which a woman feels out of control of in day-to-day life, or perhaps by disturbing memories of past events that intrude on her here-and-now life. To learn to sit with uncertainty by experiencing it in terms of what might happen in a Women's Group meeting is more productive than a contrived discussion on the topic, as she actually *feels* in that moment how uncertainty feels for her when perhaps a member is missing, or she is unsure and so anxious regarding how what she is just about to disclose for the first time might be received. She experiences in action how it feels to put her trust in others enough to break her 'Don't be close' rule. Others maybe reflect back to her how she works so hard to justify her absence to illness, or that she truly could not afford to attend the last meeting because of an unexpected bill, not because she had been gambling; all because she is so used to the impact of her gambling addiction being that she is not trusted by others who know her. This *in action* quality of Women's Group is a vital component to keep. It is a microcosm of thinking, feeling, relationship and living a life in action. The healing and the long-term recovery lie in using the space to identify, through self-reflection and reflection in the mirrors held up by others in the Women's Group, the situational, psychological and emotional triggers for gambling addiction, which lie in relationship with oneself, with others in Women's Group and so with others in the outside world. *Always* with the intention that all of this rich information, this rediscovered joy, the fear and pain of the rich 'jam sandwich' of truly intimate relating and authentic expression of herself, should be put into practice *outside* of Women's Group for Problem Gambling. That is the way to best ensure she will reach a position of needing neither gambling addiction nor Women's Group as a way to avoid her fears of truly living a life.

Chapter 8

For the practitioner
What makes a Women's Group therapist?

> The therapist's character is a predominant factor in successful therapy; the therapeutic impact that has been attributed to the therapist's personality factors has been reported to be eight times greater than that associated with treatment technique.
>
> (Lambert, 1989)

We have now worked through the experience of what it is for a woman to be a member of Women's Group for Problem Gambling with all of the challenges to be met and rewards that are to be gained if she faces her fears and stays with working on her relationship with herself and with others. We have looked at the assessment process for potential Women's Group members, but when establishing a Women's Group for Problem Gambling, equally as vital is to ask the question: What is it that makes an effective Women's Group therapist? A formal therapeutic training and qualification is of course necessary, as is extensive experience of one-to-one counselling and therapy, or ideally group process. The art of holding in mind at one and the same time the surface level conversation between up to seven Women's Group members, while interpreting what the subtext of the interaction might be, making possible links with what is being said or not said with patterns of gambling addiction, takes time to develop. A sound understanding of gambling addiction is essential, therefore, along with the differences in male and female gambling patterns. Women with gambling addiction know that their addiction is not the same as addiction to drugs or to alcohol and in many cases they know it because they might have had substance addiction problems before. They know too that their form of gambling, the experience they crave from gambling, is different on the whole from that sought after by men who gamble addictively, although there are some cross-over points (Karter, 2013), they will swiftly know through watching and listening whether their therapist understands this too. They on the whole will be exhausted and frustrated from attempts in the world outside to explain that their addiction *is* an addiction, it is not just about greed for money, and why they cannot 'just stop', and they are more likely to be open to disclosure if they feel the therapist already understands the dynamics of their addiction, and this can be conveyed in early meetings by using any appropriate opportunity to demonstrate this understanding, through perhaps reflecting on how even if there is a win, it is probably unlikely that they would have walked away with the winnings, because they were maybe just buying time in the gambling experience. Anything that conveys a true empathy with how a woman might be feeling before, during and after gambling will help to create a strong working alliance. The empathy does have to be true; however, women with gambling addiction are women who have survived often damaging relationships and life experience and have become used to lying and manipulating to meet their cravings for their addiction; they are particularly watchful, intuitive and perceptive, and vigilant to any form of disingenuous behaviour.

My experience, too, is that Group members are more likely to trust in the therapist if they imagine through what they see or intuit that their Group therapist is someone who has a little life experience, bearing in mind that in Women's Group for Problem Gambling we are likely to encounter stories of the destruction and pain that life and relationship can bring, the desperate lengths that members have been driven to as a consequence of their gambling. We will hear that they have begged, stolen, borrowed, sometimes sold their bodies and would have offered up their souls to get money to gamble or keep loan sharks and payday lenders at bay. They will talk of the demands of juggling being mother, daughter, wife, partner or professional and the pain and depression of grieving for lost opportunities to the preoccupation of gambling addiction. They will often grieve for the loss of time more than for the loss of money. Time is the greatest loss to gambling addiction and sadly the one that can never be recouped. I have heard women reflecting in Women's Group together, or in one-to-one therapy, on their perception of a counsellor or therapist whom they view as being very young or inexperienced and the tendency is towards concern that the therapist in question may not have enough experience to be able to empathise with the experiences that the women may wish to discuss. As we have heard, women who first come to Group often lack compassion and empathy for themselves, but rarely have anything but reams of both, for others. They frequently report that, when they believe that their therapist lacks life experience or is not at an age at which they imagine she might have adequate life experience, their concern with the therapist's wellbeing and with taking care of her and her feelings, then takes precedence over working on their own process, or developing their skills of expression, which they suppress to protect the therapist from what they have believed anyway to be the unspeakable shame and guilt that accompanies the stigma of being a woman with a gambling addiction. This unconsciously might be an attempt to focus on another's feelings rather than their own and so perpetuate the avoidance of self-reflection offered by gambling addiction. We might argue, and in one sense rightly so, that this is all grist for the mill of the therapeutic setting, but it is important too, that as the potential therapist we are entirely honest with ourselves in terms of our limitations and whether we feel that we are as yet resilient enough to withstand the challenges of Women's Group work. We ourselves need to be able to tolerate all the emotions that the women themselves are learning to sit with: anger, sadness, anxiety. We need to be comfortable also with humour and playfulness as a part of the process. Yes, the issues that arise during Women's Group process are often deep and dark but there are moments of genuine humour too, and an ability to be playful is one of the joys that comes as a woman leaves gambling addiction far behind.

One of the greatest challenges that the Women's Group therapist faces is that of being the source of so many transference projections. The therapist will, as within any other therapeutic group, represent mother, teacher, the manager in the workplace and all that multiplied by seven members in the Women's Group, all with their own expectations, based on their individual experience, to transfer onto their therapist. In that way, in one and the same Group, as therapist we might be loved and hated, glorified and vilified, warmly welcomed in or rejected subtly or openly. We need to be able to tolerate this and to be with our own sense of disappointment, rejection and our fears of uncertainty.

> Louise had joined an established Women's Group at the five-month period. At the end of her first Women's Group meeting, having said she might come back the following week as she had gained a lot from listening to other Group members, she then turned to me and with intensity, anger and dislike in her voice, said, 'But you, I'm not sure about you. Everybody else talks about themselves, you just talk about us (Group). I'm not so sure I like you. What's your role here?' Louise, I knew from her referral and assessment, had a very difficult relationship with her very controlling mother, who never drank, smoked or gambled but would tell Louise she should just

stop gambling, not understanding how very difficult this was never having had to give up anything for herself. I knew that Louise was likely to be transferring her expectations of her mother on to me, that because I did not join in with the open self-disclosure in Women's Group that I was as her virtuous mother; there to judge her and lacking in true empathy. The professional part of me understood that process, yet the part of me that has personal feelings was hurt at Louse's rejecting words and did not like not being liked. I was worried for the consequences of her words on the other Women's Group members and how that might impact their perception of me. My seven years' experience as Women's Group therapist and twelve years in clinical practice has enabled me to quickly recognise and to separate my personal feelings and my professional thoughts and response, so I was able to manage to remain in my professional self.

Becoming 'mother' for Women's Group is, as we might expect, a natural transference and with that will be transferred all of the hopes and dreams for the nurturing and care a woman perhaps never received from her natural mother and so too disappointment when we let her down. She may transfer too, as we saw in the vignette above, all of the anger that she feels towards the absent mother, the controlling or abusive mother; the mother who stood by and allowed her to suffer at the hands of abusive others. Gambling addiction has been in many ways a substitute attachment, a stand in for the parental attachment that was broken or just never even formed in the first place. The slot machine, computer screen, or that of her Smartphone, her tablet, is always there to help her manage distressing feelings by playing them away, and along with them, the feelings that she has towards the mother who has let her down by not originally providing the warmth and care to hold her in her painful feelings, to teach her that it is possible to tolerate emotional pain, so that she does not need to turn to the warmth offered by the bright lights, the warm colours of gambling to soothe her. As gambling addiction has been a substitute for mother, as recovery from gambling addiction moves on, the substitution of mother moves on, then to the therapist. Feelings about rejections, abandonments, betrayals by mother, which have been suppressed by gambling, are often intensely expressed at that time and, if so, may be aimed at the therapist. Again, whatever the personal feelings and urges to react, both the personal and professional self of the Women's Group therapist must be resilient enough not to shrink from the anger, or to rise to attack back, but to invite healthy expression of anger, while being curious about its true origins, and to help the Women's Group member to understand what and whom it might truly be about; perhaps it does belong with the natural mother, or with those who have not met her needs for care and comfort. At times when her anger might indeed be about therapist error, then having the courage to stand and face the fact that we as therapists are human and will make mistakes will reap more rich rewards than hiding behind the right to therapist nondisclosure. If she can trust us to say when we have got it wrong, she is much more likely to trust that, actually, sometimes we might just get it right. She will know too, as do not we all, that it does take courage to face mistakes that we have made and the possible judgements that will accompany disclosing them. If we as therapist can do so, then we model an essential life skill for recovery from gambling addiction and that is facing reality even when it is not a pretty sight. We model too that it is possible to tolerate uncomfortable feelings and not be destroyed by them. We have a chance to engage in conflict resolution in action. There is so much to be gained therapeutically for bringing our real self, there in the moment, into Women's Group meetings.

As Women's Group therapist, as well as drawing mother transference, very often we might experience a mother countertransference. For any of us reading this chapter who are not trained therapists, countertransference is anything that the therapist might feel in response to their client. When working with gambling addiction, we will so very often be working with women who are very much caught in a stasis of a childlike way of being. No matter how great a woman's responsibilities, or how proficiently she carries them through, within the professional workplace, or as mother, wife, partner, the part of her that got trapped into gambling addiction is the vulnerable Child inside of her that is frightened of being fully present and engaged in either her inner or outer world outside of the sealed and suffocating bubble of gambling addiction. If she has lived through, as have so many women with gambling addiction, abuse in childhood, as have 85 per cent of the Women's Group members I have met since 2006 (Karter, 2013), then even more so as the fear she will have experienced will have made any rich inner growth extremely hard, as all of her attention would have been on the outer world, scanning for danger in order to survive. Depending on our response to childlike qualities of dependence, fear of abandonment, the need to please, or the desire to rebel, we will as Women's Group therapists have our own response to the Child in the women with whom we work through Group process.

Leigh was three months into Women's Group. She had been gambling on slot machines in AGCs for ten years and was now three weeks into recovery. She had shared with Group that when she was

> as young as five years old she and her younger sister had been taken to the casino by her mother, who had developed a gambling addiction to slot machines, following the sudden death of Leigh's father. Leigh had silently cried as she told us that she remembered feeling so frightened because her mother would disappear for hours and, although in the same casino, she could not find her mother and often it would be security guards who would find Leigh and her sister and take them to their mother. Leigh was now in her late thirties, a highly skilled professional and had been married for several years, but for her the hardest part of recovery was constantly feeling empty and completely alone in the world without the feeling of being safely wrapped up in gambling addiction. At the end of the meeting in which she had shared this, Leigh and I shared a moment of direct eye contact, Leigh had said nothing while she continued to weep, but her eyes desperately held onto mine and reflected her sheer terror. I felt Leigh was that little girl again, pleading with to me to rescue her.

Working as a therapist within Women's Group we will many times have the strings of our hearts pulled by stories of just how vulnerable a woman has been throughout her life because it was exactly these kinds of situations that scared her into taking flight to the relative safety of gambling addiction. We will hear too, the consequences of gambling addiction, and often it is especially the devastating debt she has created in buying her escapism, have locked her into the most tortuous traps. Her desperation for money may not end when the addiction to gambling ends, debt may take years to pay off and this can leave her vulnerable to more than the risk of relapse to gambling. It might be very hard to hear, and not be able to rescue her from, the fact that when she leaves Women's Group that evening she might be returning to live with and sleep with the man who abuses her but she is afraid to leave, not only because her self-confidence is shattered, but because she does not have money to support herself and, as a result of preoccupation with gambling or the lies she has told, she has no friends or family who will shelter her. Or we might hear from the woman who has borrowed money that she cannot hope to pay back and that those she had borrowed from then continue to abuse the power and influence she perceives it gives them over her and her debt is being paid in sexual favours, which sicken her and leave her valuing herself less and less each time it happens. Or the woman who borrowed £200 from a loan shark, whom she has now paid four times over, but still he threatened to burn her alive in her home if she does not make another payment.

> *If you owe money to the bank, you make a payment plan. You owe money to a friend or your family, they have power over you.*
>
> (Jane, 45 years old. Playing slot machines and online bingo for 20 years)

At these times we may feel strong urges to rescue the woman, to go into the 'doing' something about it, because it is easier than being with her feelings about it and of course our own. It is of course absolutely appropriate to refer her to agencies that are able to help her, or to express concern, or to strongly suggest that she acts swiftly to change her situation, but it is our role always as therapist to encourage her to develop her own inner resources, to empower her to be able to act outside of Women's Group as she grows a stronger Adult self.

For some of us as therapists, understanding from some textbook learning that 'gamblers lie and manipulate', we may be vigilant to this happening in Women's Group for Problem Gambling. In the early meetings sometimes lies might be told as trust at this point is still at a fragile stage of development. A woman may lie to conceal the fact that she has no money to travel to Group that week because of a relapse to gambling. On the other end of the spectrum, she may lie about events that have happened that week, embellishing them in detail because she fears she will not be interesting enough if she does not wear a mask of woman in crisis. Depending on our own life experiences of being lied to, being betrayed and even our own experiences and feelings about uncertainty, we will react to this in individual ways. Our internal responses may range from anxiety about how to manage this hunch that she is lying, to fear, irritation and even anger that she is manipulating Women's Group and us in such a way. We might be tempted to take a tough love approach and to say that we see what is going on and that lying will not be tolerated, that we are there in Women's Group to be honest with each other and yes the latter part of that statement would be absolutely right, a purpose of Group is certainly to learn to look at the truth beyond the denial of addiction. Our strong response however might come from our anxieties and our anger at having been lied to in the past by others we are close to, or our need to take control of the situation, both personally and professionally, but might not be in the long term the most productive way of doing so and of encouraging her future honesty within Women's Group. For any of us, if we tell lies, it is as a defence mechanism; she is lying because she is afraid of attack should the truth if she tells it does not 'Please others'. If we can allow her to lie, conscious of the fact that she is doing so and being curious about why she feels this necessary, but continue to foster an atmosphere of unconditional positive regard, her defences are much more likely and naturally to be lowered. If she is in denial of the reality of her situation this is because she does not yet feel she has the inner strength to look in the mirror and face what it is that she sees reflected back. Remember, if we have one year to 18 months, we have time.

There is a balance to be attained in our way of being and in suggesting that we are empathic and demonstrate Unconditional Positive Regard (Rogers, 2003). I do not suggest that there is never a time to be firm and there will be many challenges to our resolve and boundary keeping and, as we have discussed, Women's Group will be reassured by our doing so. Sometimes there is need to protect the Women's Group space from a woman's family and friends who might wish to enter the space, curious to see what takes place, or concerned when they see changes in her that they did not expect and maybe do not even like, and wanting to see what it is that happens in that mysterious one and a half hours. . . . Sometimes a woman's friends and family sign her up to stop the gambling behaviour, but do not sign up for other changes that will occur throughout the process as she works on the underlying causes of her gambling addiction, changes such as her becoming more assertive, not always 'Pleasing others' to the detriment of herself, and so then wonder at the healthiness and helpfulness of Women's Group. She may in part wish to please and appease the people who want to attend a meeting. Let us remember that regaining trust is always a key issue after gambling addiction and she might imagine that proving her attendance and hard work, or her family having a conversation with me, would help this. She may be so used to being reduced to Child by guilt or controlling others that she cannot conceive of saying 'no' to such a request. If we model protecting the space and allowing no observers in, it is an example to her that our boundaries – both personal and physical – are important, and that we do not have to allow others to cross them just because they wish to do so. Another time when I have found through experience of my practice that it is rewarding to be persistent and encouraging is if an established Women's Group member is considering leaving Group prematurely. Of course we must respect the wishes of any client, but remembering that it is the childlike, fearful part of any of us that is hooked into addiction, so too it is likely to be that part of us that wants to run away from all that is feared in Group meeting. If a woman wishes to leave, I strongly encourage her to return. I try to talk with her, we look at her fears, I encourage her to go beyond them because this is going beyond gambling addiction and miles down the path of recovery. More often than not this is all that is needed and most women do return because, in discussing their fears, we contact their Adult rational self that has the courage to come back into Women's Group and work on their fears, and in Group women who return never speak of anything but being glad about that fact that I did not let them run away easily.

All throughout the Women's Group process we, as the therapist, are paying attention not only to the interpersonal in intrapersonal dialogues for each woman in Group, but need also to pay keen attention to our own. This will feel easier if we are more naturally familiar with our own psychological, emotional and somatic responses, to be familiar with what signals to us that we are caught in our own Child responses triggered by the fear of the sometimes intense emotions that will be expressed in Women's Group and sometimes towards us as Group therapist. To undertake our own therapy before and if necessary during taking on the responsibility of facilitating Women's Group meetings will help us to identify those times when we are inwardly reacting from our own Child and help us, in spite of this, to respond from an Adult place of professionalism.

Regular clinical supervision is crucial to remaining objective and to ensure that as Women's Group therapist we are not getting transformed into the shape that the Group may wish us to become as they project their fears and desires onto us. If the supervisor has a sound understanding of gambling addiction, and the gender difference issues inherent in the issue, then so much the better. Projective identification, the feelings on behalf of the client – feelings of which they are unconscious themselves – is something that we might expect to strongly and regularly experience. The purpose of gambling addiction in women is to suppress uncomfortable feelings and so it is not at all uncommon as therapist to leave a Group meeting, in the first couple of months especially, feeling a level of anger, sadness or anxiety that puzzles us because we are pretty sure that it is not our own.

As the Group progresses, and if the therapist is working in the way just described, which is from a core of boundaried professionalism, but as an authentic, feeling and expressive being, willing to engage in the process of relating, as time passes it can become increasingly hard, and at times even frustrating, to be a part of the growing warmth and connectedness that is there amongst the Group members, but having to keep a distance to maintain professional objectivity and to continue to provide a strong therapeutic presence. As women become gambling free and underneath are revealed as often wonderfully warm, humorous, smart and resourceful characters, there may be times when it might be so tempting to make a personal disclosure when asked about our life outside of Women's Group, because we wish somewhere inside of ourselves on a personal level that we could truly be friends with these women with whom we work so hard to develop relationships and yet with whom we must always to an extent hold our whole selves back from. We are working within a group, and in Chapter 1, we explored how our natural instinct is to belong, to become a part of a group, and as Women's Group therapist, we are in that way going against our nature because we may not 'Please others' if we do not share our personal information, or we may not belong if we turn down the invitation to join the Group members for coffee after the meeting. It is a sacrifice we must make in order to fulfil our role. We must find a way to be as fully present as possible within the Women's Group meetings and to appropriately disclose our considered thoughts and feelings about what is occurring within the process, but to accept that we have limitations to how much we might join in the process of growing intimacy. That if we have had a bad day, no matter how much we might long to share a little of that with Women's Group at check in, no matter how much we might long for a little of the warmth and support and compassion we see offered amongst the women we share Group with, no matter how much we would love to truly develop friendships, it is unfair to burden the Group with our needs. We must always hold our place in Women's Group, as being both within and without, knowing that sometimes we will be glad of the boundaries and element of professional distance we maintain from being without, as it helps us to have a clearer perspective. Knowing that, and sometimes too, we might be a little sad and frustrated by the limitations that stop us from developing the kind of attachments we see growing week by week within the group.

It will be easier to resist this temptation to overstep our relational boundaries and let our personal needs override our professional responsibilities, if our needs for friendship, warmth and support are being met in our lives outside of Women's Group for Problem Gambling. The role of Women's Group therapist is a thoroughly rewarding one, but also can be draining, so it is vital that as therapist we are having our resources replenished not only in good clinical supervision, but in our personal lives, too. Ensuring that we have a balanced life, full of friendship, family and experiences of belonging to social groups of all kinds will help us to feel held and supported and cared for, and too give us an empathy with how very wonderful and how very difficult it can be to belong to any of these groups. We will be more fully behind our words when we encourage women to develop and live the adventure of a life outside of the hermetically sealed bubble of gambling addiction, if we ourselves live life outside of the Group and of our work, which could just as easily become a safe haven from engaging with our own life in the world outside, and with ourselves in relationship to others.

What we model in terms of a way of being is being observed at all times in Women's Group. So many of the women we will meet have had inadequate parenting, lacking both in modelling or in education regarding self-care, and through the preoccupation with their gambling addiction have left not only their intolerable thoughts and feelings behind, but have become almost disembodied beings; both slot machine playing and online gambling and gaming adding to the sense of being able to transcend not only the reality of their life in the real world but their own physical self. Often I have heard women addicted to slot machines speak of the relief associated with being able to be taken out of oneself, to stand in front of the slot machine and leave all anxieties behind as they absorb themselves in the game, to be able to pretend that they were somebody else. To those around them in the AGC, the bingo hall, they were nobody, and so could pretend that they were anybody, somebody without the misery of a life they were leaving behind in their addiction. The virtual self that one can create in some online gambling games now adds to the desired feeling of becoming disembodied and increasingly detached from reality and able to take on a persona completely removed from the authentic self, which the woman affected by gambling has been struggling to leave behind because to be fully present in herself carries too much risk of fear, or pain. The result we know impacts her mental and emotional health, but also her physical wellbeing. She maybe has not seen a doctor or dentist in years, taken no exercise, taken no pride in her appearance as though her physical self were screaming out what her hidden addiction concealed so well; the fear and pain that she struggled under the burden of. Some women I have met have hesitated about coming to their first Women's Group meeting because they feared how they would be judged by others for the lack of care that they have paid to their physical self. Eating disorder can sometimes be the cause of this concern over physical appearance, and is a common comorbidity among the women I treat for gambling addiction, and there are strong similarities in the underlying motivation and the effects of overeating: 'Eating may gratify the need for some sense of soothing through taking in particular foods that symbolize comfort, or through further disassociation from feelings' (Heenan, 2005, pp. 9–10). With anorexia too, we might recognise patterns akin to gambling addiction: 'Many people shudder at the thought of anorexia and obesity. It is a small madness to keep the other madness at bay' (Woodman, 1982). Other links between gambling addiction and eating disorder are that with both there is the important factor of changing for what is perceived to be a positive way a psychological and emotional state without the feared feeling of being physically out of control, as with substance abuse, and both can be seductive for the level of secrecy that is possible. Coming into Women's Group for Problem Gambling it will be harder to keep secrets about any other ways of surviving life.

> *For Karen, for whom the anorexia that had been her battle since being abused by her uncle at the age of 17, there was the fear of being seen as so painfully thin in Women's Group. Following inpatient treatment, Karen had maintained a healthy way of eating for several years, but having become desperately unhappy in her marriage to a controlling husband she developed a gambling addiction to slot machines in casinos to control her intolerable thoughts and feelings. When the debts spiralled out of control, her anorexia returned as an attempt to control the anxiety triggered by gambling addiction. By the time of entering Women's Group for Problem Gambling, Karen had her eating back on track, but felt ashamed of her still thin appearance and feared the other Group members would guess her secret and reject her for it. Again, we see the fear of being different equating with the fear of rejection.*

Often, we might see this pattern of managing the anxiety and depression caused by gambling addiction with alcohol in male clients, and with women I frequently see eating disorder used in a similar way as for Karen. When working with women and gambling addiction, one of the first signs of sound recovery is when a woman begins to be aware of her physical self and attends medical and dental appointments and maybe values herself enough to buy some new clothes or have her hair done, just as when we were following the Women's Group process, we saw Sarah had done. This is more than mere vanity; it is also about a woman recovering her self-esteem and recognising who she sees reflected back to her when she looks in the mirror, as well as acknowledgement of the fact that she belongs to a wider community and that she is seen by others within it. If we, as therapist, arrive at Women's Group meetings having had a good sleep, having valued ourselves enough to take regular exercise and having taken a general pride in our appearance, we are modelling this way of being to women who have almost forgotten their physical self existed, so absorbed have they been in their gambling addiction or dealing with the high anxieties of its aftermath.

In the opening paragraph to this chapter it is suggested that it is the therapist's character that has been found to be the most important factor in affecting change. While we are exploring the character of the therapist, it might be valuable to ponder the question I was recently asked, which is would it be possible in my professional opinion for a man to take the role as therapist in Women's Group for Problem Gambling? Clinical experience strongly suggests that women in addiction respond more positively to a woman counsellor or therapist but, as there are no comparative Women's Groups for Problem Gambling, there are of course none as yet, either, that have male therapists. I therefore must answer this question based on the findings of my practice in relation to the women who have attended Group meetings and the themes that have consistently arisen since Women's Groups began in 2006. Reflecting on both the issues underlying gambling addiction and the issues that are the consequences of gambling addiction, I think and feel that it is of the greatest benefit to the individual woman and to Women's Group as a whole, if the therapist is also a woman. Were I to say anything different, I believe too, that I would be contradicting what I have put forward in this book and in my previous book *Women and Problem Gambling* (Karter, 2013), which is that that there are gender differences inherent in gambling addiction and in the way men and women think about, feel about and engage in relationship with themselves, with others and life in general, and that in order to become our most authentic and fully functioning self, those differences should be honoured and celebrated, not repressed. A male therapist is able to empathise with the issues concerning women, such as being daughter, mother, professional woman at work, the demands a woman feels to be all these things, yet he can never truly *feel* and so understand on the deepest empathic level, how it is to live these, any more than I might ever *feel* truly what it is to be son, father, the professional male at work. The women who attend Women's Group will be aware of this and, as we have explored, a key role of therapist in Women's Group for Problem Gambling is modelling a way of being, managing and thriving in life; if a woman is therapist, this also gives Group a way of being to aspire to.

In Chapter 1 of this book, I described that the idea of a women's group for gambling addiction was born out of the need that my women clients were feeding back to me: the lack of support acknowledging the differences in male and female gambling addiction mode and motivation, but also the discomfort that they felt in predominantly male peer-support or therapeutic groups. Let us reflect for a moment on what we understand to be the recurrent themes of Women's Group: abuse in childhood, domestic violence, acts such as prostitution or being pressured into sexual acts to repay debt, causing shame and potentially a block to attending that very first meeting in Women's Group. Yes, we might argue that many women also have issues of trust and betrayal involving other women, which may for similar reasons make the Women's Group process with a woman as a therapist feel like hard work on a transferential level, but the highly sensitive issues that are discussed in Group meetings, sometimes of a sexual nature or of highly intimate issues of female physicality, make it feel more comfortable to do so in a women-only group. Women consistently report in Women's Group and in one-to-one that they believe they would not disclose more sensitive issues connected to being a woman with gambling addiction if there was a male presence either as a peer or as therapist. If we are to work holistically, as I have found reaps such a bounty of rewards for ongoing recovery and a healthy productive life, I believe we need to make it as easy as possible for a woman to bring her whole self to Women's Group. Another question, which arose off the back of the original that I answer, was: How does it help the lonely and isolated woman to learn to develop relationships with men of a romantic or sexual nature if she attends a women only therapeutic group? As we have discussed, very many of the women who attend Women's Group for Problem Gambling do have issues of trust with men and if a woman is heterosexual, the deeply damaging experiences that she has survived are likely to have affected her ability to be intimate to any degree with men, and yes, the loneliness and isolation factors of feeling unable to choose to take a life partner do leave her open to relapse to gambling addiction. If she is bisexual or lesbian, then she may find that any rejection, abandonment or being shamed by her family or social group for her sexuality – and perhaps for her, too, isolation and loneliness as she fears 'coming out' – are a motivation for her gambling addiction. One of the aims of Women's Group for Problem Gambling is to help women to learn more about themselves; what it is that caused them to be in the previous, or current, destructive relationship patterns, not only with addiction but with others. Many women find that through this they gradually learn to trust *themselves* again. This, therefore, is invaluable in itself to a woman's confidence in allowing herself to be close with men, as even though she may not be able to guarantee her trust is safe in the hands of her new partner, she can trust enough in herself to recognise the signs and to remove herself if her physical self or her psychological or emotional world is under threat.

If we return once again to the quote at the beginning of the chapter, not only from this research evidence, but from years of anecdotal evidence and what I have been taught by the women with whom I have met, therapist character I would agree is the predominant factor in treatment outcome. We do still, however, need a therapeutic technique and having one helps us not only to progress the treatment of the Women's Group, but helps to give the therapist something sound to be grounded in and on, to lessen the risk of falling in and becoming lost in the Group process; to help us to maintain our place in the Group meeting of being at one and the same time inside and outside.

The therapeutic models that I use within Women's Group for Problem Gambling are those that I use within one-to-one therapy, and those are elements of the Person Centred model (Rogers, 2003) and Transactional Analysis (Berne, 2010). The Person Centred model core conditions of Unconditional Positive Regard, Congruence and Empathy I have found to foster a sense of trust and respect amongst Women's Group members. As we touched on earlier, in the early stages of Group meetings, we might expect to be lied to, we may feel manipulated, as these are the consequences of gambling addiction, and for the woman who has been gambling for many years this will be an ingrained pattern of behaviour, as she has learned to hide her addiction and to get her cravings met by manipulating money to gamble for fear of the consequences of being open and honest. If we can show her respect and remain always curious to the reason for her behaviour, she will lower these understandable defences, we will understand her better, and therefore through reflecting what we see, help her to understand herself. If we can be congruent, we demonstrate that it is possible and desirable to experience the whole range of human emotion and to express rather than suppress feeling, with gambling addiction.

In Transactional Analysis, we have a meaningful, easily communicated and understood language to explain the inner conflicts that a woman experiences. We can help her to understand that the Adult part of herself rationally knows that the only way out of her trap is to stop gambling, to learn to relate and to get well, to grow up and sometimes to please herself before others and not always work so hard, that it is impossible and misery-making to try always to be perfect, that to be strong we need to be able to feel and to be close. That if we are to be healthy and whole, we need *relationships* with others. In Women's Group, there in action we will see, and through the language of Transactional Analysis, can help a woman to understand how the Child part of herself fears punishment, the searing pain and anxiety of abandonment, rejection, separation and loss, feeling shame and guilt if she takes that risk of letting go of her attachment to gambling and developing in its place that which is her greatest fear, but all that she has truly always wanted and that gambling addiction has helped her to deny she needed, for all its up and downs; that is the warmth and comfort, the delights and laughter, the support through pain and tears that is truly authentic, healthy, human relationship.

References

American Psychiatric Association (2005). *Diagnostic and statistical manual of mental disorders (DSM-IV), 4th edition*. Washington, DC: American Psychiatric Association.

American Psychiatric Association (2013). *Diagnostic and statistical manual of mental disorders (DSM-5), 5th edition*. Washington, DC: American Psychiatric Association.

Basham, P., & Luik, J. (2011). *Gambling: A healthy bet*. London: Democracy Institute.

BBC Online (2013). 'Web re-defining human identity says chief scientist'. Available at: www.bbc.co.uk/news/technology-21084945 [Accessed December 2013].

Berne, E. (2010). *The games people play*. London: Penguin.

Bowlby, J. (1951). *Maternal care and mental health*. World Health Organization Monograph (serial no. 2).

Bowlby, J. (1986). *Attachment and loss, vol. 3: Loss, sadness and depression*. New York: Basic Books.

Bradford Cannon, W. (1915). *Bodily changes in pain, hunger, fear and rage: An account of recent researches into the function of emotional excitement*. New York: Appleton-Century-Crofts.

Briere, J. N. (1992). *Child abuse trauma*. London: Sage.

Channel 4 (2012). *All in the best possible taste with Grayson Perry*.

Clarkson, P. (2003). *The therapeutic relationship* (2nd edn). Oxford: Wiley-Blackwell.

Dowling, C. (1982). *The Cinderella complex*. New York: Pocket Books.

GamCare (2013). Available at: www.gamcare.org.uk/data/files/ANNUAL_REVIEW_aND_PLAN_9_NOV.pdf html [Accessed December 2013].

Gambling Commission (2013). Gambling participation: Activities and mode of access. Available at: www.gamblingcommission.gov.uk/pdf/Gambling%20participation%20-%20activities%20and%20mode%20of%20access%20-%20April%202013.pdf [Accessed December 2013].

Gambling Compliance (2013). 'Online games driving problem gambling among women' Available at: www.gamblingcompliance.com/node/51290 [Accessed December 2013].

Harkaway, N. (2012). *The blind giant: How to survive in the digital age*. London: John Murray.

Heenan, C. (2005). A feminist psychotherapeutic approach to working with women who eat compulsively. *Psychology: Journal Articles (peer-reviewed). Paper 12*. Available at: http://digitalcommons.bolton.ac.uk/psych_journalspr/12 [Accessed 30 March 2014].

International Center for Media and the Public Agenda (ICMPA) in partnership with the Salzburg Academy on Media & Global Change (2010). *The world unplugged: Going 24 hours without media*. Available at: http://withoutmedia.wordpress.com/ [Accessed 21 March 2014].

Jeffers, S. J. (1997). *Feel the fear and do it anyway*. London: Rider and Co.

Karter, L. (2013). *Women and problem gambling: Therapeutic insights into understanding addiction and treatment*. Hove, UK: Routledge.

Kross, E., Verduyn, P., Demiralp, E., Park, J., Lee, D. S., et al. (2013). Facebook use predicts declines in subjective well-being in young adults. *PLoS ONE*, 8(8), e69841. doi:10.1371/journal.pone.0069841

Lambert, M. J. (1989). The individual therapist's contribution to psychotherapy process and outcome. *Clinical Psychology Review*, 9(4), 469–485.

Lips, H. (2006). *A new psychology of women*. New York: McGraw Hill.

Mountain Dreamer, O. (2006). *The invitation*. Dorset: Element.

Newman, R. (2012). 'Appy and you know it?'. *London Evening Standard* (3 August). Available from: www.standard.co.uk/lifestyle/esmagazine/appy-and-you-know-it-8001503.html [Accessed 8 March 2014].

NHS (2013). *Gambling addiction*. Available at: http://nhs.uk/Livewell/addiction/Pages/gambling addiction.aspx [Accessed November 2013].

Rogers, C. (1951/2003). *Client-centered therapy: Its current practice, implications, and theory*. London: Constable & Robinson Ltd.

Sartre, J. P. (2001). *Being and nothingness*. London: Routledge.

Smith, M. K. (2011). Young people and the 2011 'riots' in England – experiences, explanations and implications for youth work. *The Encyclopedia of Informal Education*. Available at: www.infed.org/archives/jeffs_and_smith/young_people_youth_work_and_the_2011_riots_in_england.html [Accessed December 2013].

The Times (2013). 'Stress hits the middle class mothers'. Available at: www.thetimes.co.uk/tto/life/families/article3696964.ece [Accessed December 2013].

Vlahovic, T. A., Roberts, S., & Dunbar, R. (2012). Effects of duration and laughter on subjective happiness within different modes of communication. *Journal of Computer-Mediated Communication*, 17(4), 436–450. doi: 10.1111/j.1083-6101.2012.01584.x

Woodman, M. (1982). *Addiction to perfection: The still unravished bride (studies in Jungian psychology by Jungian analysts)*. Toronto: Inner City Books.

Index

Note: Group members are listed by name. see 'members' for full list

abandonment. see separation, rejection, abandonment and loss
absenteeism 66–8, 71, 73–8, 86, 127, 142. see also attendance
abuse in childhood. see childhood abuse
acceptance 37, 57, 58, 81, 92, 99
action quality, women's group 50, 52, 70, 92, 110, 128, 133
adult gaming centres (AGCs) 13, 41, 109, 125, 131, 132, 139, 145. see also arcades
adult self 133, 141–3, 147, 149; growing into 126–7; initial group meetings 38–9; midway group meetings 67, 87, 92, 93, 95, 96; post-women's group 106
advertisements, gambling-related 107–9
aggression, and anger 53
Alcoholics Anonymous 25
ambivalence: dependence-independence 14; endings 92; letting go 116; women's group attendance 30, 122, 131
anger 102; and aggression 53; emotional expression 29; and engagement 127; loss 57; meeting cancellations 66; midway group meetings 49, 51, 52; moving towards closure 88–9, 91; relapse prevention 110–11; theme 52–3; therapist 141, 143; towards gambling industry 73; towards therapist 74, 137–8
anonymity 71
anorexia 17, 145, 146
anxiety 2, 3; and alcohol use 146; childcare issues 61–2; and gambling behaviour 12; holistic approach 111; initial group meetings 26, 27, 35; isolation/loneliness 13; money issues 62–3; moving towards closure 88, 95; technology withdrawal 11; uncertainty 4, 59–60
anxious attachment 51, 53
appearance, physical 145, 146
arcades 13, 54, 71. see also adult gaming centres
assertiveness, learning 53, 82, 97, 142
assessment for client suitability 118–22
attachment 41, 42, 124; anxious 51, 53; and attendance 127; and gambling behaviour 116, 149; healthy 14; initial group meetings 22–3, 27, 28; midway group meetings 66, 71–2, 73; moving towards closure 79–80, 81; needs 12; theme 47, 53–4; and trust 122; virtual relationships 9, 11. see also friendships; relationship
attendance: except if physically ill 28, 129; maintaining 121, 122, 123. see also absenteeism

attention-seeking 105–6
authentic adult self. *see* adult self
authority figures 37, 74, 91, 117, 121, 131
autumn season 62–3
avoidance 8, 16, 27, 80, 89, 90, 137. *see also* denial

baby, having another 64–5
Basham, Patrick 108
'be' rules for living: careful 38; perfect 38, 80, 85, 149; strong 6, 18, 38, 44–5, 54, 57
Beddington, Professor Sir John 10
'Being and Nothingness' (Sartre) 7
belonging: injunctions 38; needs 3, 4, 6, 7, 9, 11, 13, 15; sense of 48, 70, 123, 127. *see also* 'don't belong' rule
bereavement 14, 56. *see also* separation, rejection, abandonment and loss
betrayal of trust 8, 15, 18, 141; initial group meetings 33–4; theme 44, 46–7, 54–5
The Blind Giant (Hardaway) 3
blocking out feelings. *see* suppression of feelings
body language 9, 10, 48, 90, 105–6
bonding. *see* attachment
borderline personality disorder 24, 118
boundary-setting 2, 11–12, 91, 132; therapeutic relationship 84, 116–17, 144
Bowlby, John 6, 14
break-up of gambling relationship 108, 109. *see also* pain of withdrawal
bullying: childhood 16; online 8
bureaucracy/form-filling 117, 123

cancellation of meetings 66–7
Carina (women's group member) 115, 116
case studies. *see* members
Cath (women's group member) 103–4
celebration, moving towards closure 93–4

chaotic thinking 61, 122
characteristics, therapist. *see* therapist characteristics
checking in 29–39, 48, 49
childcare issues 61–2. *see also* custody of children
childhood abuse: sexual 8, 63, 65, 95, 108; theme 16, 17, 24, 31, 90, 147
child-like states 15, 18, 139–40, 142–3, 149; attention-seeking 105–6; dependence 126–7; midway group meetings 65, 74; moving towards closure 92, 93; theme 44, 59. *see also* 'don't grow up' rule
choice: empowerment 31, 83, 96; fear-based 15; healthy 44, 56, 59; and freedom 46. *see also* control
Christmas time 63–5, 66, 125
Citizens Advice 112
Clara (women's group member) 128–9
Clare (women's group member) 16, 101
client suitability, assessment 118–22
clinical supervision, therapist 143
closure. *see* moving towards closure
coffee shops 7, 9
comfort eating 145
comfort zones, moving outside 26
commitment to group 22, 30
co-morbidity 17, 145
communication, non-verbal 9, 10, 48, 90, 105–6
compliance 16, 95. *see also* deference
confidentiality 28, 30, 33, 118, 125
conflict resolution 3, 9, 11, 51–2, 139
confronting the problem 3, 18, 79. *see also* facing feelings; mirror to the self
congruence (genuineness) 42–3. *see also* adult self
contract, group 27–8, 29, 124
control, being in 3, 13, 17, 132; anger 53; eating disorders 146; of finances 45–6; initial group meetings 26, 37; by others 46, 49, 56, 82–3, 91; and uncertainty 88. *see also* empowerment
coping strategies 17, 35, 130

Index 155

counselling, prior to women's group meetings 21–2
countertransference 139
cravings: gambling 36, 56, 59, 62, 79, 87, 92, 106–7, 131, 136, 149; love 108; mother figure 44; technology 11
creativity, and gambling 32
cross addiction 16, 25, 32, 82
cultural background, clients 119
custody of children 25, 32, 34, 43, 95, 100, 118

Dawn (women's group member) 71–3, 77, 83, 90, 94
debt. *see* money issues
defences 112, 142; intimacy 72; loneliness 6–7; separation/loss 89–90. *see also* avoidance; denial
deference 15. *see also* compliance
denial 57, 89, 141, 142. *see also* avoidance
dependence. *see* independence-dependence
depression 2, 3, 12, 13, 35, 88, 101, 128–9; alcohol use 146; holistic approach 111; separation/loss 57, 65; suppression of anger 73; technology withdrawal 11
desire to please. *see* 'please others' rule
difference/diversity 4–5, 9, 119
direct contact, therapist 127
disappointment: meeting cancellations 66–7; midway group meetings 74; moving towards closure 90–1; relapse 99; theme 55; therapist 137
disclosure. *see* self-disclosure
disconnection from feeling. *see* suppression of feelings
distance, therapist 143–4
distancing: from gambling environment 110; online 8–9
distraction techniques 24
diversity/difference 119
domestic violence theme 16, 17, 147
'don't be' rules for living 37
'don't be close' rule for living 38, 132; loss 57; midway group meetings

50–2; moving towards closure 80, 92, 96; relapse prevention 112; theme 53–4. *see also* attachment; intimacy
'don't be important' rule for living 37, 48, 131. *see also* empowerment
'don't be well' rule for living 38, 87–8, 105
'don't be who you are' rule for living 37, 58–9
'don't belong' rule for living 38, 50, 52. *see also* belonging
'don't feel' rule for living 38, 54, 57, 92. *see also* suppression of feelings
'don't grow up' rule for living 37, 87–8, 105, 126. *see also* child-like states
'don't think' rule for living 38, 48
'don't tell' rule for living 38, 43, 46, 77, 80. *see also* self-disclosure
drivers, transactional analysis 38
DSM-Diagnostic and Statistical Manual (American Psychiatric Association) 120
duration, women's group 124–5

eating disorders 17, 145, 146
education about gambling 69–70
empathy 42, 43, 144, 147; moving towards closure 92; online distancing 8; recovery 108; therapist 84, 122, 136–7, 138, 142; women's 34
employment 82, 83, 99, 101–4
empowerment, group members 14, 31, 46, 65, 141. *see also* control; 'don't be important' rule for living
endings, fear responses 92. *see also* moving towards closure
engagement in therapy 116–17, 122, 127, 128
escapism 15, 72, 83, 108, 109, 115, 140
exclusion. *see* separation, rejection, abandonment and loss
exercise, taking regular 146
expectations of women's group 129–30, 137
eye contact 9, 10–11, 140

face to face contact 9, 10
Facebook 10
facilitators, group 16. *see also* therapist
facing feelings 11, 42–3, 130, 131, 137, 149; engagement 128; moving towards closure 93, 95; post-women's group 101, 103; relapse prevention 110–11. *see also* suppression of feelings
facing mistakes, therapist 139
facing the problem 3, 18, 79. *see also* mirror to the self
failure injunctions 37
fallibility, therapist 74, 139
family: groups 3–4, 6; history 23–4, 25, 65, 75, 87, 91–2; happiest and unhappiest memories 119–20, 121
fear/fear of: endings 92; freedom 5–6; and maintaining engagement 128; mental health service 117–18; moving towards closure 85–6; punishment 149; triggers 51. *see also* fight, flight or freeze responses
feedback questionnaire 99–102
Feel the Fear and Do it Anyway (Jeffers) 28
feeling being, therapist as 84
feeling injunctions 38
feeling marginalised 131
feeling trapped 46, 49, 56. *see also* control; empowerment
feeling unwanted. *see* separation, rejection, abandonment and loss
feelings: about therapist 90–1; tolerating 42–3, 44, 137, 138. *see also* facing feelings
fees, group 126–7. *see also* money issues
fight, flight or freeze responses 23, 29, 51, 104, 128, 140; moving towards closure 85–6, 88
finances. *see* money issues
follow up appointments 98–9
form filling, therapist 117, 123
fragmentation, group 13
freedom and responsibility 5–6

friendships: with therapist 143–4; women's 34, 42, 54–5, 94. *see also* attachment; relationship
furnishings, meeting room 130–1

Gamblers Anonymous 15
*Gambling: A Healthy Be*t (Basham & Luik) 108
gambling behaviour 21–2; education about 69–70; motivation 1, 16–18, 22, 96, 101–2, 106, 149; online 11, 12, 13, 25, 41, 110, 145; and social/ socioeconomic groups 4, 6, 13, 119. *see also* adult gaming centres; triggers; withdrawal; women's groups for problem gambling
gambling industry 73, 107–8
GamCare 112
garden metaphor 97–8, 105
gender: and gambling patterns 15–16, 135, 146, 147; therapist/therapeutic groups 147, 148
genuineness 42–3. *see also* adult self
getting on with life 102, 103
Google search engine 9
Gordon Moody Association 113
greed for money 17, 43, 46, 136
grieving 57, 136. *see also* pain of withdrawal from gambling; regret
group: identity 4–5, 6, 13; women's. *see* women's groups for problem gambling
growth 59, 126, 139
guilt. *see* shame/guilt

happiest and unhappiest memories 119–20, 121
Hardaway, Nick 10
having another baby 64–5
having something to lose 104
healing 80, 93, 133
health injunctions 38
healthy relationship 95, 96, 97, 98, 110, 149; therapeutic 116
Helen (women's group member) 111; initial group meetings 24, 31, 37; midway group meetings 47, 50, 69, 70, 71; moving towards closure

86–8, 89, 91, 92, 94, 95; seasonal effects 63–4
here-and-now relationships 77, 78
holistic treatment model 111
honesty 126
humour 71, 137, 143, 149

identity: gambling 31, 39, 41, 58, 141; group 4–5, 6, 13; mental health service user 35; mother 50, 62, 64–5; professional 35, 36–7, 89–90, 96
illness, missing the group through 28, 66, 129
impulse control disorders 120
independence-dependence 14–15, 19, 105; child-like states 126–7, 139; and gambling behaviour 115, 116
indications, joining women's group 118–22
industry, gambling 73, 107–8
initial group meetings 21–3; checking in 29–39; group members 24–9
injunctions, transactional analysis 37–8. *see also* rules for living
inner child. *see* child-like state
inner city: gangs 6; life stresses 119
inner voice 2, 15, 48, 83
insecurity 33. *see also* separation, rejection, abandonment and loss
internet. *see* online
interpretations, therapist 16, 89–90
intimacy 148; defences 72; therapeutic relationship 90, 144; women's group 50–1. *see also* 'don't be close' rule for living; sexual relationships
invitations to join women's group 118–22
isolation. *see* loneliness

Jane (women's group member) 141
Janet (women's group member) 34, 43, 100, 101; betrayal of trust 54; Christmas time 65; initial group meetings 25, 32–3; midway group meetings 49, 50, 73, 75; moving towards closure 86–7, 90, 92, 94, 95–6

jealousy 33
Joanna (women's group member) 128–9
joy 137; of relationship 79–80
judgement, fear of 116, 119. *see also* non-judgementalism

Karen (women's group member) 146
Kross, Ethan 10

labels, gambling 28, 35, 46
leaving the group prematurely 66–8, 71, 73–8, 86, 127, 142
Leigh (women's group member) 139–40
length/duration, women's group 124–5
letting go 81, 116, 149. *see also* moving towards closure
Level Ground private practice 118
lies. *see* secrecy/web of lies
life after women's group 97–112; Cath 103–4; feedback 99–102; follow up appointments 98–9; gambling-related advertisements 107–9; Rebecca 105–6; relapse avoidance/prevention 104–7, 109–12; Sarah 100–2, 103
life experience, therapist 136–7
listening without interruption 31
Little Red Riding Hood story 97
London: riots 6; women's group clients 119
loneliness 3, 23, 28, 51, 57, 86, 97; Christmas time 65; defences against 6–7; and gambling behaviour 18; Leigh 140; relapse 105; sexuality 119; and social networking 13; suppression of feelings 53–4. *see also* separation, rejection, abandonment and loss
loss. *see* separation, rejection, abandonment and loss
Louise (women's group member) 137–8

maintenance work, relapse avoidance 104–5
male gambling patterns 15–16, 135, 146, 147

male therapists/therapeutic groups 147, 148
Marcia (women's group member) 126
Maria (women's group member) 139
mask of problem gambler 39, 41, 58, 141
meeting cancellations 66–7
meeting space 25–6, 130–1
members, women's group. *see* Carina; Cath; Clara; Clare; Dawn; Helen; Jane; Janet; Joanna; Karen; Leigh; Louise; Marcia; Maria; Paula; Rebecca; Sarah; Terri; Veronica; Zara
memories, happiest and unhappiest 119–20, 121
mental health problems 24, 35, 87, 108, 117–19
microcosm of life, women's group as 23, 119, 124
midway group meetings: absence/leaving 66, 67, 68, 71, 73–8; education about gambling 69–70; meeting cancellations 66–7; new members 70–3, 77; rejection/abandonment feelings 64–5, 75–6, 78; seasons/Christmas 61–6; withholding disclosures 67–9
Mind organisation 113
mirror to the self 79, 112, 122, 133, 142
misinterpretations 16
modeling life skills 4, 82, 84, 139, 142, 145–7
models. *see* therapeutic technique
Money Advice Service 113
money issues 115, 128–9, 136, 140–1; anxiety 62–3; control by others 46, 82–3; Dawn 71–3; facing the problem 79; group fees 126
mother: identity 50, 62, 64–5; role of therapist 45, 74, 138–9
motivation, gambling 1, 16–18, 22, 96, 101–2, 106, 149
moving on 103. *see also* life after women's group
moving towards closure 79–94, 110; Helen 95; Janet 95–6; Paula 89–90, 92, 94–5; Sarah 96
music 94

Narcotics Anonymous 25
National Problem Gambling Clinic 113
needs 2, 147; attachment 12, 53; belonging 3, 4, 6, 7, 9, 11, 13, 15; relationship 19, 149; therapeutic 118–19
new members, midway group meetings 70–3
no, saying 83
non-judgementalism 18, 43, 145
non-verbal communication 9, 10, 48, 90, 105–6
NSPCC Adults Abused in Childhood 113
numbing. *see* suppression of feelings

Ofcom 107
one-to-one appointments 98–9
online: bullying 8; distancing 8–9; gambling 11, 12, 13, 25, 41, 110, 145
openness 43, 118, 129
over-compensation, childcare 62

pain: tolerating 29; of withdrawal from gambling 57, 108, 109, 110, 116
parents, supporting 6
passivity 15, 83, 87
Paula (women's group member) 34–5, 101; Christmas time 65; holistic approach 111; initial group meetings 23–4; midway group meetings 47, 50, 67–8, 68, 69, 71, 75; moving towards closure 89–90, 92, 94–5; uncertainty 60
peer support groups, limitations 16
perfectionism 38, 74, 149. *see also* 'be perfect' rule
Perry, Grayson 4
person-centred model 42–4, 149
personal agendas, initial group meetings 30–1
personal growth 59, 126, 139
personal qualities, therapist. *see* therapist characteristics
personal space, respect for 90
personality disorder 24, 118

physical appearance 145, 146
physical intimacy 90
playfulness 80
'please others' rule for living 2, 16, 30–1, 34, 128–9, 142; and anger 52–3; Christmas time 66; injunctions 38; inner child 139; life after women's group 102; moving towards closure 80, 82, 83, 85, 95; themes 43, 45, 46, 48; therapist 144; uncertainty 77
post traumatic stress disorder 24
practitioner. *see* therapist
pride in appearance 146
problem resolution 127. *see also* facing the problem
professional identity 35, 36–7, 89–90, 96
professional qualities, therapist. *see* therapist characteristics
professional support, relapse prevention 111–14
projections 123, 131
projective identification 143
prostitution 43, 136, 147
punctuality 127
punishment: fear responses 149; relapse prevention 110

qualifications, therapist 135
qualities, therapist. *see* therapist characteristics
questioning, Socratic 68
questionnaire, feedback 99–102

rape 24, 69, 95
Rape Crisis England and Wales 113
real life concerns 80–1
reasons for gambling 1, 16–18, 22, 96, 101–2, 106, 149
Rebecca (women's group member) 105–6
rebellious inner child 139
recovery 72, 81, 96, 104, 142; follow up appointments 99; and gambling-related advertisements 108. *see also* relapse
referral, to support agencies 141
reflection 10

refreshments 47, 49, 126
Refuge organisation 114
regret: childcare 62; Christmas time 63; facing the problem 79; relapse prevention 107; theme 57–8
regularity, venue and meeting times 130
rejection. *see* separation, rejection, abandonment and loss
relapse 46, 56, 128–9; Christmas time 66; life after women's group 99, 104, 105, 106–7, 109–12; moving towards closure 86–7, 94, 95; support for prevention 111–14
Relate organisation 114
relational skills, learning 42, 75, 81, 82, 97, 128
relationship: being fully within 19; healthy 3, 12, 22, 95, 96, 97, 98, 110, 149; joy of 79–80; midway group meetings 70, 72, 77, 78; with members outside women's group 128–9; needs 149; poor 1–2; real-world 11; sexual/romantic 79–80, 148; virtual 7–10, 11, 13, 41, 145. *see also* attachment; friendships; therapeutic relationship
religious background, women's group clients 9, 119
remorse 107. *see also* regret; shame/guilt
re-parenting 18
respect: gaining 95; for personal space 90; unconditional 44. *see also* unconditional positive regard
responsibility: and freedom 5–6; taking 76–7, 93, 123
risk, therapy 116
Rogers, Carl 42
romantic relationships 79–80, 148
room/meeting space 25–6, 130–1
routine, safety of 102, 122, 130
rules for living. *see* scripts/rules for living
rules, women's group 27–8, 29, 42
running from the group 29

sadness 42–3, 63, 65. *see also* regret
safe space 55, 92, 111, 130

Samaritans 114
Sarah (women's group member)
  35–7, 54, 56; Christmas time 65–6;
  initial group meetings 25–9; life
  after women's group 100–2, 103;
  moving towards closure 82–5, 94,
  96; midway group meetings 48–50,
  69, 75, 76
saying no 83
scripts/rules for living 2, 4, 16, 37–8,
  39. see also 'be' rules; 'don't' rules;
  'please others'; 'work hard' rule
search engine, Google 9
seasons, effect of 61–6, 125
secrecy/web of lies 2, 3, 12, 18,
  42, 125, 136, 149; initial group
  meetings 31; labels 46; therapist
  responses 141. see also self-
  disclosure
secular society 9
self-blame 77
self-disclosure 34, 41, 44, 45, 112;
  confidentiality 118; therapist 143–4;
  withholding 51, 67–9. see also
  'don't tell' rule
self-empathy 43
self-esteem/self-worth 46, 47, 52, 58,
  116, 146
self-harming behaviour 17, 23, 95
self-medication, gambling as 61, 111
self-soothing 2, 70; eating 145;
  gambling behaviour as 107; relapse
  prevention 110–11
self, women's group as mirror 79,
  112, 122, 133, 142
separation, rejection, abandonment
  and loss 4, 11, 18, 22–3, 116, 146,
  149; absence/leaving the group
  75; Christmas time 65; defences
  89–90; inner child 139; learning
  to cope with 124; midway group
  meetings 49–50, 51, 64–5, 68–9,
  75–8; mother identity 64–5;
  moving towards closure 79, 81, 87,
  88, 91–3; of self 2; Terri 49–50,
  58, 64, 68, 75–7, 121; theme 56–9;
  therapist issues 137; withdrawal
  from gambling as 57, 108, 109,
  110, 116; Zara 126–7

sexual abuse 8, 63, 65, 95, 108
sexual relationships 79–80, 148
sexuality: women's group clients 95,
  119, 148
shame/guilt 2, 12, 18, 116, 142;
  attendance 129; childcare issues
  62; Christmas time 65; follow
  up appointments 99; life after
  women's group 104; and life
  experience of therapist 137;
  midway group meetings 51, 64, 72;
  moving towards closure 82, 83, 95;
  theme 43, 46, 47, 56
Simms Social site 12
single mothers 6
sitting position, choice of group
  members 27
social networking 7–12
socioeconomics, group membership
  4, 6, 13, 119
Socratic questioning 68
song-writing 94
soothing. see self-soothing
space, therapeutic 25–6, 130–1
starting up a women's group 115–33;
  assessment for client suitability
  118–22; boundary-setting 116–17,
  132; confidentiality 125; duration
  of group 124–5; engagement
  116–17, 127, 128; fees 126–7; group
  contracts 27–8, 29, 124; mode of
  functioning of 129–30; therapeutic
  relationship 116–17; venue 130–1
stealing 43, 62, 104, 115, 125, 136
strength/'be strong' rule 6, 18, 38,
  44–5, 54, 57
stress 1, 5, 13, 27, 35, 83, 95, 103,
  119, 132
stuckness 18
substance addiction 117, 135, 146
suicide attempts 8, 106, 125
summer season 61–2
Sun and the North Wind story 41–2
supervision, therapist 143
support, relapse prevention 111–14
suppression of feelings 15, 28–9,
  36, 43, 79, 143; anger 52–3,
  73; disappointment 55; and life
  experience of therapist 137; loss

Index

56–7; midway group meetings 68, 77; and relapse 110. *see also* 'don't feel' rule
survivors 80
Sussex, women's group clients 119
symbolism of the totem 4

TA (transactional analysis) 37–8, 149
tearfulness 149; betrayal of trust 54; feedback 100–1; initial group meetings 29–30; midway group meetings 50, 76; Sarah 37
technique. *see* therapeutic technique
technology 7–12. *see also* online
Terri (women's group member): absence/leaving the group 66–9, 71, 73–7, 127; attachment 53; initial group meetings 24, 32, 34; midway group meetings 47, 48, 49–50, 52, 67–8, 73; moving towards closure 84; separation, rejection, abandonment and loss 49–50, 58, 64, 68, 75–7, 121
text message reminders 122, 123
theft 43, 62, 104, 115, 125, 136
themes 41–52, 127, 132; abuse in childhood 16, 17, 24, 31, 90, 147; anger 52–3; attachment 47, 53–4; childlike states 44, 59; disappointment 55; domestic violence 16, 17, 147; pleasing others 43, 45, 46, 48; regret 57–8; relationship 42; separation, rejection, abandonment and loss 56–9; shame/guilt 43, 46, 47, 56; trust issues 44, 46–7, 54–5, 59, 132; uncertainty 59–60, 132
therapeutic relationship 18, 28, 116–18, 122; boundary-setting 144; maintaining 123, 127, 128
therapeutic technique 148–9; holistic approach 111; person-centred model 42–4, 149; transactional analysis 37–8, 149
therapist: control 91; error 139; interpretations 16, 89–90; modelling life skills 4, 82, 84, 139, 142, 145–7; training 135

therapist characteristics 84, 135–49; life experience 136–7; personal needs 144; and transference 137–9; warmth 117, 143, 144
therapy: engagement 116–17, 122, 127, 128; prior to women's group 21–2
thinking: injunctions 38; time 10
time of year 61–6, 125
timeframes, women's group 124–5
tolerating: feelings 42–3, 44, 137, 138; pain 29. *see also* facing feelings
totem, symbolism of 4
tough love 45, 141
training, therapist 135
transactional analysis (TA) 37–8, 149
transference 33–4, 118, 121, 131, 137–40, 148
transparency 43, 118, 129
trapped, feeling 46, 49, 56. *see also* control; empowerment
travelling home alone, anxiety 62–3
treatment models. *see* therapeutic technique
triggers: anger 53; defence mechanisms 88
triggers, gambling 24, 32, 43, 44, 52, 69; exposure to 79; feeling infantilised/trapped 46; gambling-related advertisements 107–9; insight into 92–3; life after women's group 103; mode of functioning of women's group 130; moving towards closure 87, 89; relapse prevention 106–7, 110; stress 83; time of year 125; uncertainty 51
trust 18, 19, 39, 41–3, 132, 133; attachment 122; building 44; initial group meetings 21, 23, 31, 33–4; labels 46; meeting cancellations 66; moving towards closure 81, 91; sexual/romantic relationships 148; themes 44, 46–7, 54–5, 59, 132; therapeutic relationship 118; and therapist characteristics 139, 142; tolerating feelings 45. *see also* betrayal of trust

uncertainty 4, 42, 116, 132; anxiety 59–60; and control 88; fear of 18; initial group meetings 26; midway group meetings 77; moving towards closure 87; separation anxiety 59; therapist 137; tolerating feelings 45, 51; themes 59–60, 132
unconditional positive regard (UPR) 42, 43–4, 142, 149
understanding: motivation for gambling 149; therapist 117, 136–7. *see also* empathy

venue 130–1
Veronica (women's group member) 108–9
violence, domestic 16, 17, 147
virtual relationships 7–10, 11, 13, 41, 145
voice, inner 2, 15, 48, 83

warmth, therapist 117, 143, 144
web of lies. *see* secrecy/web of lies
websites, professional support 112–14
weed metaphor 97–8, 105

withdrawal from gambling behaviour 11–12, 22; pain of 57, 108, 109, 110, 116
withholding disclosure 51, 67–9. *see also* 'don't tell' rule
witnessing 11, 15
Women and Problem Gambling (Karter) 115, 147
women's friendships 34, 42, 54–5, 94. *see also* attachment; relationship
women's groups for problem gambling 14, 15, 19; action quality 50, 52, 70, 92, 110, 128, 133; contract 27–8, 29, 124; dynamics 21, 22, 111, 121; indications for joining 118–22; mode of functioning 129–30; ninth week 47–52; rules 27–8, 29, 42. *see also* initial group meetings; members; midway group meetings; moving towards closure; starting up a women's group; themes
'work hard' rule for living 38, 43, 46, 63

Zara (women's group member) 126–7